THE PARENT'S GUIDE TO

COACHING SOCCER

John P. McCarthy, Jr.

BETTERWAY BOOKS

CINCINNATI, OHIO

97 96 95 94   5 4 3

Library of Congress Cataloging-in-Publication Data

McCarthy, John P.
  A parent's guide to coaching soccer / John P. McCarthy.
    p.   cm.
  ISBN 1-55870-144-3 (pbk.)
  1. Soccer for children—Coaching. I. Title.
GV943.8.M36   1990
796.334083—dc20   89-29912
                                                        CIP

Cover design by Sandy Conopeotis
Typography by Park Lane Associates

Betterway Books are available at special discounts for sales promotions, premiums and fund-raising use. Special editions or book excerpts can also be created to specification. For details contact:

Special Sales Director
Betterway Books
1507 Dana Avenue
Cincinnati, OH 45207

To Mike Christy for suggesting I coach;
to Bob Walsh and John MacIvor for coaching with me;
to Roy Dyer for his advice;
to the boys and girls and parents who hung in there
through rain, mud, heat, and cold;
to my family;
and to the spirit which moves all of us to challenge life.
This book is ours!

CONTENTS

PREFACE

"Hey Coach, I can't make baseball practice tomorrow because I have a soccer game, okay?"

I looked down at the robust freckle-faced kid, and I remember wondering what this red-blooded American boy saw in soccer.

That was 1978, not so long ago. My attitude reflected the ignorance of an entire generation of American parents. We grew up in a culture where football was the number one game. I had no idea what soccer was really about. I knew it was played all over Europe, and I figured Europe would come to our way of thinking sooner or later. It was a dark age here for soccer, and I was a dinosaur.

A few years later, my daughter developed an interest in playing sports. She tried a year of baseball, but never really got into it. Our town had just started a soccer team for girls a bit older than my daughter. I called the president of the local soccer club and asked why there was no team for younger girls. He said, "There is no coach." I answered, "You have a coach now, what do I do?" He said, "Get on the phone and put together a team." A month later we were on the field.

Fortunately for me, none of the girls had ever played soccer. They never knew how little I knew and neither did their parents. I had coached and played other sports, so I could fake it, but I really knew nothing. Little did I know that I was on the threshold of my most rewarding coaching experience, and that I was about to become part of one of the greatest games in the world. The soccer explosion of the 1980's is clear testimony to its growing popularity.

I figured the first step was to get a book on soccer. As stated in my earlier book *A Parent's Guide to Coaching Baseball*, there were plenty of baseball books, but none that really helped the novice. Well, what I found when looking for something on soccer was even worse. I couldn't find any books at all.

Fortunately, there were coaching clinics available through our state soccer organization, and I learned the fundamentals. But there just wasn't anything that really brought the concepts of soccer home to me, or that clearly showed me how to develop a kid's skills. I felt very much alone. Most coaching materials assumed that the reader had played the game. But, like most American parents, I had not.

I knew then that we needed a book dedicated to parents, one which understood that most parents have no experience with the game. Well, here it is! I hope it helps you and your child, and more important, I hope it strengthens the relationship you share.

How did my girls do? We lost our first game 17-0, against a team that had been together for three years. So I set our goals realistically. The next game we decided to keep the other team below ten goals, and we succeeded. Then our goal was to score, and we succeeded. Finally, our goal was to win a game, and we were successful at that also. Two years later the girls went undefeated, and then became the first-ever girls varsity team at Hillsborough High School in New Jersey. Then I dropped down to coach my younger son in soccer for a few years. During my years coaching soccer I played the game myself on weekends, pick-up games for coaches and parents at our high school field. It is hard to learn a sport as an adult, but the skills are slowly coming. I learned a lot, it's all here in this book. Good luck with it.

To Kids,
Jack McCarthy

1.

KNOWING THE BALL

The most important thing you can do as a parent is to encourage your child to spend time with the soccer ball. A comfortable relationship between the player and the ball is what soccer is all about.

More important to a child's success with the game than size, speed, or innate athletic ability is oneness with the ball.

Physical ability can help, a lot, but there is little you can do about what your child was born with, beyond some conditioning. *Nonetheless, you can teach soccer skills and ball control.* These things alone, if practiced, will make children good enough to contribute significantly to their teams and feel good about themselves.

Most youth soccer players begin by being "prisoners of the ball." Their entire focus is on the ball itself. They are, in effect, trapped by the ball, not yet comfortable with it. It slows them down, makes them feel awkward. Sometimes, they just want to kick it away in frustration. The *only* cure to this is practice. Eventually, ball control becomes natural. As this happens, their focus will expand from the ball itself and open up to the field around them. With this comes confidence and the true enjoyment of the essence of soccer, team play. But until they *know the ball,* until they can move freely and gracefully with the ball, able to focus only a portion of their concentration on the ball and the rest on the field of play, until this occurs, the ball is like a great weight around them.

My daughter did not have great speed, but she worked at her skills and became an excellent soccer player, winning state-wide honors. She played intelligently, but most important, she *knew* the ball and developed confidence in her ability to control it. The great news to parents is that this can be learned, so it can be taught.

GETTING THE FEEL OF THE BALL

The key to the game of soccer is ball control, particularly at the younger ages where game dynamics and team play are learned only very slowly. A boy or girl who can move with the ball will be most valuable to the team. Ball skills are essential and fundamental. They include trapping (receiving passes), juggling, heading, faking, dribbling, passing, and shooting the ball. We will discuss each in detail. They *must* be practiced, the more the better. They can be practiced alone or with a parent or friend. Remember, as a parent you can give pointers and, even more important, encouragement. You can get some needed exercise yourself and build a more solid relationship with your child.

However, before we get to specific skills, let's talk a bit more about a most basic thing in soccer—getting the "feel" of the ball. The concept is a psychological one. Young players must perceive the ball as if it were actually a part of their foot, or connected at least by an invisible string. For instance, the foot shouldn't really *strike* the ball when dribbling, it simply "carries" the ball along like another big toe. The way to develop this perception is to have the ball around as much as possible, and just fool around with it. I know there is a time and place for everything, but some excellent young players keep a ball under their homework desk and just roll it under their feet as they study.

Having a ball around as much as possible is an emerging concept in world soccer circles, and is now being taught by many coaches around the world. Several years ago my wife's cousin started a soccer camp and flew in some English coaches to instruct. They conducted a coaches' clinic, and we were told that continual *contact* with the ball is the key to developing skills.

The technique is very simple; put the ball on the ground, and fool around with it. The great thing is that your child doesn't need a lot of space, only a few square feet. Repeatedly touch the ball, alternating feet. Roll it around, jump over it, roll it around the outside perimeter of each foot, back and forth under each foot, kick it back and forth between each foot, speed up, slow down, just keep fooling around! Get to know how the ball feels against each part of the foot and how it reacts. This can be done in the yard, or in the cellar on a rainy day. It can be done in any room except the ones mom says are off limits. (See Figure 1.)

One thought is to keep a soccer ball in the family or recreation room and suggest that your child fool with it while sitting, watching TV. Don't encourage kicking or dribbling, just gently roll the ball around, back and forth, faster and faster, under each foot. Make it a game or a challenge. Count the number of times the child can move the ball back and forth between the legs, or the number of times the player can jump, even jump rope, with the ball locked between the feet. Another drill is to jump and touch the top of the ball with the bottom of one foot, alternating feet, trying to increase speed all of the time.

The main idea here is constant touching, rolling, and shoving to develop a "feel" for the ball, getting to know the ball.

I met a number of foreign coaches over my years coaching soccer—English, German, South American. They all say that this ability to move "around" the ball, and to feel and to know its contours, its reaction to touches and nudges, is critical to executing ball control skills. It's important, so it's the place to start.

THERE ARE NO LEFT FEET

Many of you may be more familiar with basketball than soccer, and will appreciate the value of being able to dribble and shoot with both hands. In basketball, once you know an opponent can dribble with only one hand, and can dribble the ball only in one direction, then you can cheat a bit to that side as you defend against that other player. However, someone with equal skills in both hands is much tougher to stop.

So it is with soccer. A player who must rely on one foot to dribble, shoot, pass, or trap the ball is only half as good as can be. Fortunately, unlike our hands, our feet are more used to being used equally. So it's easier to get that left foot going. Stress this with your child! Coaches should also do so during practice, requiring players to do various drills left footed. You can support this while your child practices in your backyard.

If your child has a problem developing the left foot, and just

Figure 1
KNOWING THE BALL

Hop sideways over ball, alternate touching with bottom of foot

Jump with the ball between the ankles

Roll ball up the back of the leg

Just have fun with it

Figure 1 (cont.)
KNOWING THE BALL

Kick it between the feet

Roll it under the foot and around the sides of the foot

While reading a book

Just fooling around!

can't seem to focus on it, take off the right soccer shoe and make the child wear a boot (or nothing). Do this for daily for fifteen minutes or so, and use of the left foot will come around.

CONFIDENCE

It is a wonderful thing, especially for a parent who has supported his or her child's growth in sports, to watch a youngster develop. The early visions of awkwardness and frustration are replaced by ones of smoothness, grace, and confidence.

Confidence is as important in soccer as in any sport. Without it your child will not fight for the ball, will receive it without being relaxed, will not be able to make plays, and will kick the ball away prematurely. Confidence brings on the aggressiveness needed to beat an opponent to the ball. It relaxes the body and controls nervousness. It frees one to look around to see what's best to do. Confidence encourages the child to try to do something on his own, to try something new, and thus to improve individual ability.

Putting young children under age ten into full field, eleven against eleven, soccer pushes children too fast, and does not build confidence. Children don't get the ball enough, don't develop skills, and often just find themselves in a swarm of stampeding kids.

Parents, you are the best answer to this dilemma. You're not going to change the system, but you can insert yourself into it. If you play with your children one-on-one, or two-on-two, you can control their development. You can let them win a few times, at least allow enough room for confidence to grow. You also may counter any criticism they might face on the field from the coach and other kids. You can tell them that with practice they will improve, that you can guarantee it! Remind them to be patient. Not everyone can be the best, but everyone can improve. Maybe your child is content to just hang on, and that's okay too! There are plenty of other things they can choose to really work at. For children who want to be better soccer players, *they can be with practice, with your support,* and, if you can, *with your direct coaching.* Growth and improvement are not something elusive, they are natural! Improvement will occur with practice all by itself, it will occur more quickly with your help.

2.
DRIBBLING

THE HEART OF YOUTH SOCCER

Most coaches will tell you that soccer is a game of passing, and that the team that can execute a series of passes will control the ball, penetrate to the goal area, and score. They will say that too much dribbling is to be discouraged, that the percentages are higher to stop a dribble than to intercept a good pass, and that a good pass can cover a lot of distance quickly. They are generally right, but I still believe that dribbling is the most important skill, and the most fun for your child.

The passing theory doesn't work well at the youngest ages; it's not practical. At young ages, up to ten years old, a child *must* know how to dribble. Dribbling is also easier to learn. Passing skills, learning to spot an open teammate, and the ability to receive a pass come slowly. Kids who can dribble will help their teams maintain possession and score. They are the ones who will stand out in a game. Go watch any game at the younger ages. Those who can dribble do quite well.

Once I travelled with my daughter's team to a tournament in Canada. A young French Canadian girl put on a demonstration dribbling, the likes of which I've never seen. She could move anywhere at will. It was soccer at its best, and beautiful to behold.

Obviously there is a time to dribble, and there is a time not to dribble. Defenders dribble less because they must get the ball far away from the goal as soon as possible. Tell your child never to lose the ball dribbling in the defensive one-third of the field; the risk is too great. Forwards are usually the best dribblers because up close to the goal there may be no one to pass to. They are often on their own. Wing forwards must be able to dribble to advance the ball towards the corner.

Dribbling is the most fun next to shooting the ball. I believe that dribbling is the skill which should be practiced the most in the initial years, in conjunction with the ball control skills mentioned in Chapter 1. Children who are taught to dribble will, more quickly than with any other skill, progress most rapidly to the point that they contribute to the team and feel good about their play. This skill then will be a catalyst for other skills as confidence and desire for the ball grows. Plus, they will be able to move the ball to a position from which they can execute a good pass (when their teammates learn to get into position to receive a pass). Obviously, you should counsel your child against hogging the ball, and if any player consistently loses possession while dribbling, the coach will have to react. I had such a situation on my son's team with a boy named Dave. He was our best dribbler, and often could get around a defender. However, he began to rely totally on the dribble and was not developing the ability to spot open teammates. We talked about it, he worked on it, and he became a more complete player.

Unfortunately, at very young ages, the normal game strategy is what I call "swarm" soccer. All the kids chase after the ball and move up and down the field like a swarm of bees. The kid who dribbles best will control the game. Gradually, coaches get them to play position, but until then, there is often no one to pass to. So teach your child to dribble.

HERE'S HOW TO DO IT

Use Inside or Outside of Either Foot

A dribble starts with the foot closest to where the ball happens to be. (See Figure 2.) The dribbler moves the ball softly by making contact about halfway up the ball with the inside or outside of either foot. Often it will be with the outside with the foot slightly turned in or pigeon-toed, and most often the foot will be the one farthest away from the nearest defender.

Figure 2
BEGINNING TO DRIBBLE

Begin dribble with foot farthest from the defender

Contact ball halfway up with inside or outside of either foot

Keep the eyes up as much as possible

Eyes Up

It's important in dribbling to try to keep the eyes up, not down looking at the ball. The dribbler needs to be able to shift focus between the ball and the field. The idea here is to be able to see the field, the defenders, and the teammates. It's tough at first, but it comes with practice, with getting to *know* the ball. So something a parent needs to say regularly is, "Keep your eyes up." Remember, reminders such as these should be gently mentioned. It's tough at first, so be positive.

Sweep the Ball

While dribbling, the player doesn't really *strike* the ball. It's more of a gentle nudge or a *sweeping* motion. This relates to the concept about feeling the ball. The ball becomes part of the foot, and is shoved down the field, or swept as if in front of a broom. A useful gimmick to teach this concept during dribbling drills is to tell the players they should not be able to hear the foot strike the ball. When the ball is kicked, there is a clear sound from contact, since the foot and ball are together for only a split second. When the ball is shoved, or swept, the foot and ball are in contact for a much longer time, so there is no sound. The longer the foot is in contact with the ball the better it can control it. (See Figure 3.)

The thought here is that a sweep allows the dribbler to control *both* the speed and the direction of the ball. Speed is important so that the ball moves at the same speed as the player, and doesn't get out too far from the player, allowing a defender to steal it. *Directional* control allows for placement *away* from any nearby defender. Since the foot is in touch with the ball longer, it can better control its speed and direction.

Obviously, there are times the dribbler will strike the ball, particularly when there is no defender nearby and the best play is to kick the ball a greater distance and run up to it. However, the sweep is the main dribbling concept. Other terms which can be used to convey this concept to your child are: push the ball, shove the ball, carry it!

Figure 3
SWEEP THE BALL

Sweep or shovel the ball out to the side

Sweep it out to the front

In Tight Under the Shoulders

With a defender close by, usually in the beginning of a dribble, the player must keep the ball under the shoulders to protect it from the defender. This also allows the dribbler to fake and feint and to move the ball quickly in any direction. It's important to have all choices open. In close quarters, the ball must stay under the shoulders. The dribbler may push it out and away for speed only when it is safe to do so. (See Figure 4.)

Maintain Body Balance

The dribbler wants to feel balanced, his weight evenly distributed, not leaning too far forward. Sudden changes of direction, the need to fake, feint, change speeds, all require a sense of strength and balance. The ball should also be positioned, to the extent possible, on center with the body. Momentum is important, and a player always needs to feel in control.

Figure 4
KEEP THE BALL IN CLOSE WHEN DRIBBLING

Dribble in tight under the shoulders. This helps to fake

Ball in tight, maintain balance

Move Against the Defender's Direction

With the ball under the shoulders, the player has many options. The ball can be passed, kicked back to a free teammate, or dribbled around the defender. The option chosen depends on a lot of things, including how the defender is "sized up" in terms of ability and speed. Most successful dribblers start with a move against or opposite to the defender's direction. The player must always know where the nearest defender is, and which way that defender is moving. Usually, the best play is simply to move the other way, to catch the defender off balance. This means if the defender is approaching from left to right, the dribble should go left, forcing the defender to change direction and be off balance. The technique is to sweep the ball past the defender. Lift it high and wide enough to rise over an outstretched toe. Then, slide by the defender and go to the ball quickly before the player can recoup. (See Figure 5.)

Figure 5
MOVING AGAINST THE DEFENDER'S DIRECTION

Overcommitted defender approaches from the left

Move to the left, against the defender's direction

Faking and Feinting

Obviously, defenders won't make it easy for offensive players to dribble by them, particularly if their parents have read this book also! A good defensive player will not commit too early, and will not charge the ball without believing it's possible to get a foot on the ball or a shoulder into the dribbler!

So offensive players often need to make the defender commit to one direction, any direction, and then go the opposite way. This is done by faking.

Faking is the art of making a player believe you are going to move in a certain direction, thus getting that player to move in that direction while you go the opposite way. The amount of fake needed depends on how savvy the defender is. Let's look at faking and feinting in more detail.

1) Head fake. Sometimes a head fake to one side is enough to get the defender off balance. Just tilt the head to one direction. Tell your child that the defender must be made to *believe* the ball

Figure 6
FULL BODY FAKE

As defender approaches, Joe begins to fake to his left

Defender goes for it. Joe plants left foot to change direction

He sweeps ball to opposite direction with outside of right foot

Now, free of the defender, he is ready to advance or pass

will move along a certain path, so the fake must be convincing. A key here is to pretend to "pull" the defender a certain way. A good fake must *relate* to the defender; so make eye contact to help make it convincing. Then, with an explosive quickness, go the other way. The fake only gets a split-second advantage, and it must be capitalized on. The defender will recover quickly. The first stride away from the defender is therefore a key one.

2) Body fake. Usually the offensive player needs to make a whole body fake. This can be done by taking a full step in one direction, without the ball, and then moving with the other foot in the opposite direction while sweeping the ball with the outside of the foot. This fake works most effectively if the first step, the faking step, sweeps the foot *over* the ball *pretending* to hit it. (See Figure 6.)

Sometimes the offensive player needs to double fake, triple fake, start and stop suddenly, nudging the ball and controlling it with the sides or bottom of the foot. Determine the defender's balance. Make that player lean or commit one way or the other to any off balance position, then explode in the opposite direction. Again, I must emphasize the opening paragraphs of this book. The ability to control the ball, gained by countless hours of fooling around with it in close quarters, getting the feel for it, will allow your child to use it to control the defender as well.

3) Feinting. Feinting is similar to a fake, but it is more of a hesitation or change of pace. It's used when dribbling to pretend to slow down, or to simply change speeds. As with any fake, feints throw defenders off balance and slow them down so that the offensive player can move out quickly. A great feint is to pretend to sweep the ball and then to stop short, letting the defender commit to a certain direction. Sometimes it's useful just to *hold* the ball, gain time, let the defender commit first.

Sweep Out and Explode to Open Space

If there is no defender nearby, or once the defender who is nearby has been faked out, the first move is to sweep the ball into open space and then to explode to it. This first move is critical and it's important to remember that *an intensive, convincing fake must be followed by an explosive move the opposite way.* This allows the player first to capitalize on the defender's being off balance, and

Figure 7
SCREENING

Approach the ball at an angle between the ball and defender. Here defender must slow down to avoid a foul. Be sure to play the ball, not the defender

Playing ball, use shoulder, side, or rump to screen

If the arm goes up into defender it's a foul

then to get speed up to quickly advance the ball downfield or to have time to execute a solid pass. There may also be another defender upfield, so the dribbler needs to circle back into the open space created and look for a pass receiver. Dribblers should usually flow away from the pressure.

As noted earlier, a useful tip in faking and feinting is to try to get the ball up in the air a few inches. Often the defender, off-balance, will be able to stick out a toe in desperation, so if the first push by the dribbler raises the ball six or so inches, it sails over the defender's toe. Be sure to add this hint to drills which practice the body fake move.

Run with the Ball, Look to Pass

If the fake and the explosive thrust are successful then the player will have a second or two to decide what next to do. He can run with the ball towards open space if no defender is threatening and move the ball upfield a bit, or he can look for a teammate and execute a pass. The key is to get a bit of time to decide what's next. Ball skills can buy that time. Another helpful hint when being challenged by a defender is to tell your children to keep their bodies between the ball and the defender as much as possible. This is called *screening* or shielding the ball. It can buy some time for a teammate to come up and help. If the player is running with the ball, screening makes it more difficult for the defender to get to the ball without fouling. The idea is to use the body to obstruct the defender—back to defender, knees bent, rump out facing into the defender. (See Figure 7.) The arms can be out, to widen the screen, but should not be held too high.

DRIBBLING DRILLS

Several drills are great for improving dribbling skills. They can be practiced anywhere and are good for parents too. If you practice along with your children you will learn the drills with them, so you can better relate to them. You will improve too!

Figure 8
DRIBBLING AROUND CONES

Set up cones or other objects 4–5 feet apart and dribble around them

Fooling Around

We discussed this in Chapter 1, but it bears repeating. It is the best drill there is for a beginner. Just stand in a small area and practice moving quickly with the ball, using the inside, outside, and bottom of each foot. First, touch the ball, roll it, make sudden movements. Dance with it! Fool with it! After a while you can add some slight pressure by trying to take the ball away from your child, one on one.

Slalom

A popular drill is to set up six to eight cones in a straight line and have your child dribble and weave through them, circling the last cone and returning to the start. Sometimes I had my daughter weave to the end cone and then speed dribble back in a straight line. I used to measure the time it took. Kids love racing against the clock. Begin by setting your cones five feet apart, and vary the distance from time to time. Also, be sure every player practices with both feet. (See Figure 8.) If you don't have cones, use cups, plastic glasses, old milk containers, anything at all.

You can vary the drill in innumerable ways. One time you can require each player to use one foot or the insides or outsides of both feet. Several players can be on the course at one time to add to the need to be alert. Remind them to keep their eyes up!

Speed Dribble

I used to place a cone about sixty feet away, and have the players dribble to the cone and return as fast as they could. Someone would time them and they were required to remember their personal best time, and try to improve upon it. The idea is to run *with* the ball, allowing it to roll only a few yards in front of the player. Do not just kick the ball thirty feet and run up to it. Cones can be placed along the way to help limit the maximum distance of each forward sweep, and if exceeded the time should be disallowed. Tell your child to try to develop a rhythm, striking the ball with every other stride.

One on One

As skills improve, you can slowly begin to add some pressure. A good drill is to place two players, you and your child, inside a square area about twenty feet by twenty feet, or smaller. Then, just fight for ball control. If one person loses the ball outside the square, the other person gets control. This drill helps to teach *screening*, mentioned earlier, whereby the player learns to keep the body between the ball and the defender. You can also practice fakes and ball "touching" skills. Make the area larger or smaller as needed, but attempt to make it progressively smaller as skills improve. Place two cones three feet apart for goals, at each end, and play a one-on-one game.

King of the Hill

This is one of my favorites. Place all players in a square area. Everybody has a ball. Once a player's ball is knocked out of the square, that player is out. Each player must attack another ball while defending their own. Disqualify any player who does not try to attack. It's fun!

3.
JUGGLING

Juggling is the art of controlling a soccer ball above the ground, tapping it up repeatedly, not allowing it to touch the field. It teaches players how the various parts of their bodies may be used to control the ball. It is a great way to learn ball control, and is an essential drill for parents to use with their children. Juggling is probably the best confidence builder of all drills for the beginner.

Juggling benefits all ball control skills: dribbling, trapping, and passing (particularly trapping!). It also adds to quickness with the ball, and developing the kind of "feel" for the ball discussed in Chapter 1.

When juggling, the player uses the same surfaces of the body which are used to receive and control the ball. These are the upper forehead, the upper leg and thigh and, of course, the inside, outside, and top of the feet. One other surface, the chest, can be used to receive the ball, but is not very useful in juggling since it is difficult to bounce the ball up again. The tops of the shoulders are also available but are often too bumpy for good ball control.

Juggling is probably the first skill taught by most youth soccer coaches. It's easy to learn, and it's fun. I've heard that some players can juggle for hours at a time. It teaches young soccer players how the surfaces of their bodies are used to control a soccer ball, while effectively practicing these skills. Juggling teaches children how the ball reacts to contact, and it also teaches them to be alert to an errant bounce.

Figure 9
JUGGLING

Head juggling

Foot juggling

Thigh juggling

Keep the surface flat!

BEGINNING TO JUGGLE

One of my fondest soccer memories is the first week of practice with my daughter's team. We knew very little! I invited a few girls from the older team, and they put on a juggling show. The girls loved it, and tried to do a few themselves. A few years later they were showing off to even younger girls.

Just tell your child to try to keep bouncing the ball off the flat surfaces. Usually it's easiest to start with the upper legs and then move to the top of the foot. Encourage use of the forehead and inside/outside foot as soon as possible. A good beginning technique is to hold the ball between the hands and drop it onto the thigh, using the thigh to bounce the ball back into the hands. Then try to bounce it twice. Do the same with the foot. Use the hands until they are no longer needed. (See Figure 9.)

The key to juggling is to concentrate on the bottom center of the ball, and to think about making the body surface stiff and as flat as possible upon contact. Contact should be soft enough to control the ball. Try not to hit the ball too high, just up a foot or two each time. Establish a rhythm.

Players should count the number of times they juggle successively before the ball touches the ground. It's fun! The idea is to try to do "one better" than your previous record.

At first players will be able to juggle only a few times consecutively. They will improve slowly. Once they can get over fifteen to twenty, skill levels will increase rapidly. Remember, encourage your child always to do "one better" each day. Try to use all surfaces in a juggling sequence—foot, thigh, and forehead.

TEAM JUGGLING

You should practice juggling too! It's awkward at first, but you will improve! Then, you and your child can practice team juggling.

Two people can juggle one ball together, usually heading or kicking the ball back and forth. The player receives the pass, juggles to get control, and then passes the ball back. Sometimes, a child can juggle a ball off the side of the house or a wall; again the idea is simply to promote repetition. As in all sports, repetition, constant contact with the ball, is the secret to developing sound skills, and when your child is in a tough game situation, the ability to use these skills will be critical to his or her success.

RAINBOW

This is a form of juggle where players flip a ball from behind them over their heads in front of them. The method is to place the ball behind the heel of one foot. The other foot reaches behind the ball, toe down, making contact with the laces, and lifts the ball so it rolls up the heel of the front foot. Then the player leans forward and catches the ball with the underside of the front foot flipping it over the head. It's a fun skill to develop, used more for showing off than in a game. (See Figure 10.)

Figure 10
RAINBOW

Step over ball with left foot and roll it up back of leg with side of right foot

Push off with left foot and lift it quickly, kicking the ball with back of left heel

4.

PASSING

In 1985 a team of sixteen year old German boys was hosted by soccer clubs in our area and played against some of our teams. One of the boys, Peter, stayed at our home. When they played our high school team, it seemed as though they had twenty-five players on the field. There was always a group of three or four players within passing distance, surrounding our players, and they were able to move the ball at will. We all learned a lot about the value of passing the ball.

As your child gets older, and after a few years of playing, passing becomes the dominant and most important part of the game. The team that maintains possession will usually win, and passing to an open player helps to keep possession. This is where you, as a parent, come in.

It takes two to pass, two to practice passing. So, all you do is go out into the front yard, or any space about twenty or thirty feet long, and pass to each other. Move around a bit, learn to pass to the space in front of you. Talk about pass location and ball speed. It's fun, a great parent-child drill!

KNOW WHERE YOUR TEAMMATES ARE

The key to successfully passing a soccer ball is always knowing where your *nearest* teammates are. The best passers are able to "see" the playing field and know who is free.

This is not as simple as it sounds, and involves much mental discipline. There are ten field players, but the player needs only concentrate on those who are just ahead of him and those to the side. The closest players should always be in his mind because most situations require the pass to occur very quickly in order to take advantage of an opportunity or to protect oneself from a nearby defender. Therefore he needs to focus only on two or three team-mates. The remaining teammates are farther away, and can be picked up if and when needed.

Downfield players need to let players in front of them know where they are. As will be discussed later, communication on the field is the heart of both offensive and defensive strategy. It's help-ful for parents to remind their children, if the referee allows such coaching, to "know who is around you." Call it out from time to time to help your child develop the habit. It just takes a split sec-ond to pick up the location of teammates. The time to do it is when the ball begins to approach. It encourages him to begin to think about what to do if the ball is passed to him.

PASS IN FRONT OF THE RECEIVER
WITH APPROPRIATE BALL SPEED

The most common mistake in passing is passing the ball be-hind the receiver, forcing the play to slow down or stop. The error occurs when players pass *directly at* other moving players, and not in front of them. It's necessary to judge a player's speed, and get the ball to where that player *will* be.

Another common error is passing too hard, making it difficult to receive or trap the ball or entirely missing the receiver. If the pass is too soft it allows a defender time to intercept. Discuss these concepts with your child. Passes should be firm with enough speed to get to the receiver ahead of any defender. With practice, he will naturally come to understand passing speed and location.

A player needs to know the wind when passing. It's usually a good practice to keep passes low, to minimize wind interference. The wind can be a friend or a foe, and much of this depends on using it. In order to use it he needs to know which way it blows and how strong it is. Many passes are pushed out of bounds by a strong wind.

THE FOOTWORK OF PASSING

1) **Settle the ball.** Many players get excited when approaching a moving ball and try to pass it with only one touch. It is much easier to use the first touch to get the ball under control and then endeavor to pass it. Players should always first try to slow the ball down and get it in front of them, under control. Otherwise the chance of executing a good pass is quite low. Most times when a team loses possession it is because of a bad pass. Of course, there are times to run up to the ball and one-touch it, particularly when the player is under pressure in front of the goal.

2) **Hop and plant.** Approach the ball and plant the non-kicking foot up next to the ball so the toes are even with or past the rear of the ball and pointing at the target. If the plant foot is next to the ball, then the kicking foot will meet the ball at the lowest point in the kicking arc. Kids often plant the foot well behind the ball, but this lessens control and power. Planting the foot behind the ball should be done only when needed to lift the ball, causing the kicking foot to make contact on its upswing. Of course, lifting the ball is also accomplished by striking it a bit lower and by leaning back a bit. A small hop just before the foot is planted produces a useful rhythm. Practice the hop and plant. Both you and your child must get in the habit of observing where the plant foot lands. (See Figure 11.)

3) **Knee over ball, point toe down, and lock ankles.** The hopping motion helps to cock the kicking foot back in a *wind-up* for the kick. The knee, positioned over the ball, should then bend. The toe points down (instep kick), and the ankle locks and freezes. A useful technique here is to try to curl the toes down, thus helping to lock the ankle. We want the foot to make contact with the ball at the lowest part of the sweep; the sole should be about one inch off the field surface.

4) **Keep head down and look at point of contact with ball.** Players often take their eyes off the ball just as they kick, lifting the head. Instead, they should not only look at the ball, but should focus their concentration on the very spot where they will kick it, right at the center of the rear bulge, halfway up the ball. Such

Figure 11
HOP AND PLANT

A small hop as foot is planted
provides a natural rhythm

Plant foot up and to the side of
the ball

concentration is particularly important if the ball is moving, and helps to avoid poor contact. The soccer ball should move low to the ground, just a few inches above the grass. Have your child observe the height of the passes. Strike the ball is right at the bulge. (See Figure 12.) To lift the ball, strike it well below the mid-point.

5) **Inside, outside, instep?** The choice of foot surface depends on where the receiver is. Most passes use the inside of the foot. The *inside* of the foot, anywhere between the heel and the big toe, produces the most accurate passes. It is also the best to use for one-touch passes since this area is the largest surface. However, it is less useful for powerful or long passes since twisting the leg prevents the full body power from getting involved. The inside pass technique requires lifting the leg, bending the knee, toe up, and then striking the ball in front of the anklebone. The kicking leg acts as a pendulum, swinging from the hip. Avoid the tendency to lean back since that will reduce power and follow-through. (See Figure 13.)

The *outside* of the foot is used to shove or flick short passes. Contact is usually made with the side of the foot just at or below the smallest toe, usually in a flicking motion. This can be quite deceptive since it's a very quick pass, and the passer usually leans in

Figure 12
PREPARING TO PASS

Focus on point of contact at bulge halfway up the ball

Curl the toes like a fist

Knee over the ball, point toe down, and lock ankle

Keep pass low, usually just over the top of the grass

Figure 13-A
PASS WITH INSIDE, INSTEP, OR OUTSIDE OF FOOT

Strike ball between heel and big toe, lift leg, bend knee, toe up, swing from hip

Flick ball with outside of foot, just below smallest toe

Use instep, head down, knee over ball, lock ankle, toe down

Show your child exactly where to strike the ball

Figure 13-B
PASSING THE BALL

Don't lean back on inside foot pass, hinge waist, lean forward

Lean back on chip shot or pass. Chop ball with side of big toe

Don't strike ball with the toe

Follow through. Plant foot should hop with the forward momentum

the opposite direction, pulling the defender that way. Another deceptive pass is to kick it backwards with the *heel*. Just step over the ball and kick back to a trailing teammate.

The *instep* is used when power or distance is needed. Most passes are relatively short at young ages. Obviously, a long pass has a greater chance of being intercepted. However, crossing passes, passes far into the wing, clearing kicks in front of the goal, and corner kicks all usually require power and distance. The differences in technique are that the head needs to be lower, allowing more drive to the kicking foot. The leg speed is faster, more powerful, and the kicking arc (the sweep of the foot) is larger. The body hinges at the waist, the upper half snapping forward, exploding from the belly. Ankles are rigid, toes down, and the player should straighten the knee vigorously upon contact. It's helpful to curl the toes a bit, to help keep the toes down. The body leans back, a bit farther back than normal, to allow some lift to the ball. Strike with the *instep*, the lace area of the shoe.

Finally, there is the *chip* shot. This is a short pass which travels high in the air, usually just over a defender. It's often used in free kicks.

The player comes to the ball at an angle, planting the foot farther away from the side of the ball than normal, leans backwards to fully extend the kicking leg, and lifts the ball. Strike the ball low, in a chopping motion, and do not follow through. Keep the head down.

6) **Kick with leg speed.** Many kids get into the habit of kicking with a lazy foot, but the idea is to snap the foot into the ball with speed.

7) **Follow through.** We don't really strike at the ball as much as we kick *through* it, so the foot follows through its sweep in a smooth full arc. A good follow-through should pull the body forward, requiring the planted foot, the non-kicking foot, to hop a step.

8) **Now move.** Come down running; a player is not a spectator. There is no need to stand and watch the pass. *Get moving immediately*, somewhere. Move to the ball if the pass or reception was

bad, move for a give-and-go, or move to open space, anything, just get into the action.

PASSING DRILLS

A good passing drill is "name and pass." Players form a circle and pass the ball to each other. A receiving player must call out the name of someone in the circle *before receiving the pass* and then, touching the ball only once, pass it to that person. That person, in turn, must call another name before the ball arrives and pass it one-touch to that player. It is difficult, but it teaches players to look up at the field and pick out a receiver before they get to a loose ball.

Small scrimmages of three to five players each also teach passing dynamics, particularly if the players are limited to two touches each, one to trap and one to pass. This forces players to know ahead of time who is available for a pass. A one-touch requirement makes the drill even harder. Set up a few cones, or plastic glasses, a few feet apart for goals. Play yourself! These small-sided games are great fun and great practice.

Later chapters will discuss how to move off the ball and get in position to receive a pass.

5.

RECEIVING THE PASS

RECEIVING OR TRAPPING

A good reception begins with a good pass. The idea is to place the ball one to two yards in front of a running receiver. Too often the pass is behind the receiver, forcing the player to break stride to control the ball. The delay gives a defender more time to attack, so the receiver must work much harder. The terms *trapping* or *receiving* are often used alternatively. Trapping is used primarily, but I like the term receiving, since that's what we want to do.

Receiving skills are best developed by juggling the ball as described in Chapter 3. Juggling teaches the player how to use the flat body surfaces, forehead, chest, thigh, and the sides and top of the foot to control the ball. Receiving a pass requires these same body surfaces. However, there are some differences requiring additional skills.

First of all, the ball usually moves laterally, so the receiving body surface needs to be turned out to receive the ball. Juggling is up and down.

Second, the ball is moving quickly, often very fast. When it contacts the flat body surface it can bounce far away. Many times in youth soccer you will see a young player receive a pass and watch as the ball bounces twenty feet away. To avoid this the player must learn how to *soften*, *cushion*, or *deaden* the surface, retract it as the ball makes contact, and actually "catch" the ball.

Third, unlike juggling where the ball is bounced upwards, players want to control reception in such a way as to lay the ball down in front of them, ready for the next play. A player may wish to receive and pass with a single action. This is called a one-touch.

A FEW BASICS

Nevertheless, remember! *The best way for your child to learn to receive passes is to become a good juggler.* The next best way is to practice receiving passes, and this is something that needs two players, you and your child. So let's talk a few basics.

Get to the Ball

Often, very often, the pass will not be exactly to the player's foot. She will need to run to the ball. Often it's just a loose or deflected ball. The nearest players must then engage in a foot race to the ball. Winning teams are the ones that win most of these races. It's not just a matter of speed; it involves hustle, courage, and a strong determination to get the ball. *I can't emphasize enough the importance of this.* You can't emphasize it enough to your child. There are times on a soccer field when a player must run flat out as fast as possible, not as many times as you might think because body control and the need to maintain balance often requires the player to slow down a bit. However, when there is a loose ball or a pass, the idea is to go 100% and get to the ball. Players must believe they can win all balls for which they have a fifty-fifty chance. (See Figure 14.)

If the field is dry the ball will bounce higher; if it is wet it will tend to skip. Of course, you have to be aware of how the ball may be hooking or slicing, how the wind is blowing, and where other players are. There is time to look for defenders and teammates as one runs to the ball; although, as noted earlier, you always want to know where nearby teammates are. The angle and speed of the ball also need to be judged, and the final decision is which body surface to use to catch the ball, depending on the height of the ball, or the height of its bounce. All of this needs to be done quickly, but the quickest thing is just to get to the ball.

As a parent you can be helpful. Talk to your children about the importance of being aggressive when going to the ball. Don't

Figure 14
GET TO THE BALL

The moment of truth. Soccer games are won and lost depending on which team gets to the most loose balls.

be too critical when they get beaten, but talk to them, especially if they are not trying hard enough. The *showdown* drill at the end of this chapter is excellent for developing aggressiveness. It also helps them to anticipate when they will get beaten, and thus to slow down and assume a defensive posture.

Meet the Ball

Sound the same as getting to the ball? Not really. Often a ball will come right at you, but you still need to *move towards it,* particularly if a defender is approaching. How often do we see a child stand and wait for the ball, just to have another player fly by and scoop it away? The second player read the preceding paragraph, and *got* to the ball!

Figure 15
TAKE COMMAND OF THE BALL

Eyes on point of contact, balanced concentration

Take it out of the air to control its landing

Use most available surface to control the ball

Once it touches the ground, it might go anywhere

Take Command of the Ball

Often in youth soccer a high pass is allowed to bounce. Understandably, children prefer to field the ball low, with their feet. They are less confident with their upper surfaces, and are a bit timid about heading or chesting the ball. Unfortunately, bounces must go up and come down again, giving time to a defender to apply pressure. Also, bounces can be unpredictable especially if the playing surface is not smooth. The idea then is to *use* the head, chest, thigh, or even foot to stop the ball in flight and take control quickly. Take command of the ball, move towards it, take it out of the air, and go with it! (See Figure 15.)

Face the Ball and Present the Body Surface

At the right time, when contact with the ball can be made in a controlled manner, face the ball and present the body surface. The body weight should be balanced or on the non-receiving foot. Keep in mind the idea that a flat surface will control the ball. The inside or bottom of the foot will usually give the most control. Keep the toes up. The instep is used mainly for receiving high lofting passes. Catch these high balls as they drop close to the ground. When using the chest keep balance, knees bent, body arched, arms out. Remember not to arch the back too far too soon so there is still room to absorb the ball. Always keep the eyes on the ball. (See Figure 16.)

Relax at the Point of Contact

This should go without saying, but the moment of contact between the ball and the body surface requires undivided attention, balance, and concentration. Focus on the point of the ball where contact will be made; think about what direction it then should take. The idea is to relax a bit at the moment of contact. "Hurry up, then wait" is a useful coaching phrase. Too often kids will hurry the trap, get excited, and boot it away. Players should take enough time to trap well.

Figure 16
TRAPPING: PRESENT THE BODY SURFACE

Present the inside foot, keep the toe up, eyes on the ball

Present the upper thigh, keep balanced

Present the forehead, relax on contact

Present chest, lean back, leave room to lean further upon contact

Figure 17
DEADEN OR WITHDRAW SURFACE

Present the receiving surface, deaden the ankle

Then withdraw to further soften the moment of contact

Deaden Surface or Withdraw

Receiving a soccer ball is no different than a baseball or a basketball. In these sports the player learns to keep the hands soft, otherwise the ball will bounce out. It's no different, and even more important with soccer. Think of the difference when a ball hits something hard, and when it hits something soft. So, we want the body surface to be soft. Another word you can use to get the idea across is to *deaden* the surface. Describe it as letting the foot feel a bit limp, like a sack of old socks!

At the point of contact, the player actually "catches" or cushions the ball by slightly withdrawing the surface away from the ball to make it even softer. This should result in the ball dropping gently to the ground. (See Figure 17.)

Figure 18
VOLLEYS

Eyes on ball, point plant foot at target and come around quickly with instep

Lean as much as needed to get full extension on kick

Decide Where to Place the Ball

As skills improve, the ball can be dropped in different directions depending on how close defenders are and where the player wants to go. The trick here is first to know where to drop it and then *carry* the ball to that spot by angling the body surface as it traps the ball. Most often players will want to drop the ball in front of them, so this should be practiced the most.

Volley

Of course, whether heading the ball or receiving with the foot, the option exists to simultaneously strike the ball in midair to another player or into the goal. This is called a *volley*. Here the surface is not withdrawn, but actually strikes or rebounds the ball, often quite a distance. This move involves a fair amount of skill. Players are usually instructed, and should usually try, to first catch the ball, get control, and then execute the next move. However, there is a time for everything and the volley skill should be developed. (See Figure 18.)

Now Get Going Again

The last part of every play, of every move, is to get going again. Don't lose a step! Receiving the pass is only one part of a fluid action. Now the player has controlled the ball in front of him or her and must execute the next move, whether it is a dribble (see Chapter 2) or a pass (see Chapter 4). The point here is that players should be constantly in motion, especially when near the ball.

SOME DRILLS

I have mentioned a few passing and receiving drills in the prior chapter already. Here are a few more.

Wall Kicking

After juggling, this is perhaps the best drill there is for both passing and trapping skills. Find a wall—the side of a store, or a high cellar foundation. You can easily build your own: lean a piece of thick plywood against a tree, or build a frame on the ground. If you do this, dig a small trench to sink it a few inches into the ground for more support. Concrete walls are best because they give a good hard rebound. The rest is easy: simply kick the ball and trap the rebound. Pick out spots on the wall and try to hit them, then move up closer to practice receiving. Remember to use the instep, inside, and outside of each foot. Practice placing the ball at different spots on the ground after it is received. Try some one-touch action, and then go for controlled traps and passes.

If the wall is tilted back a bit, it will rebound the ball in the air. This will allow practice receiving with the higher body surfaces such as head or chest. Two people can do this, and you can make a game of it, scoring points for missed traps.

Two Person Drill

There is no substitute for practice with another player. Remember, you can go out yourself and work out with your child for twenty to thirty minutes. If you do so regularly your skills will improve too! Plus you will get some needed exercise as well as a shared parenting experience. Get about twenty-five feet apart and kick the ball back and forth. After a while you will be able to add motion to the practice. A great two person drill is to run down a field passing the ball back and forth. Try to lead each other with the pass just enough so the player doesn't have to break stride. My daughter and I used to do another drill where we would stand about two to three feet apart and just tap the ball back and forth quickly. We used to count to see how many we could get before one of us messed up.

Keep Away

I mentioned earlier the one- or two-touch passing drills, such as with players divided into two teams of two or three players each inside a square area. Count the number of consecutive successful passes, and the team with the most wins. If the ball goes outside the square due to a bad pass or a missed trap, the ball is awarded to the other team. This drill obviously is as good for receiving as it is for passing.

Showdown

The best drill for aggressiveness in getting to the ball is to have two players about thirty feet apart and throw the ball between them. As soon as it touches the ground they charge it. Make sure the ball rolls a bit so they are not coming *directly* at each other, to avoid collision. A variation is to have them stand near each other then throw the ball away from them, letting them run to it after it touches the ground. Again, this is a drill you and your child can do together, and you can control it, allowing the child to get a few to build confidence.

6.

MISCELLANEOUS SKILLS

THROW-INS

When the ball is kicked out of bounds along the sideline, the team *not* responsible for kicking it out gets possession. The ball is *thrown* back in from the spot where it went out of bounds, usually by a halfback or fullback. The referee need not touch the ball. The general idea is to throw the ball to an open player, wherever that person might be. It's preferable of course to throw upfield, usually into the wing area near the sideline to a teammate.

The reasons to throw up field along the sideline are twofold: 1) it advances the ball in the direction of the other goal; and 2) the receiver can use the sideline to shield the ball, that is, to eliminate one direction from which the defender may attack. However, remember, we primarily want to keep possession so if there is an open target, that's the best option.

Usually the wing forward will stand facing the thrower and either receive a pass to the feet or break upfield to receive a long throw. Another good play is to throw to the foot of a teammate who can simply shovel it back to the thrower. A third play is for the wing to break towards the thrower, while the center halfback breaks towards the wing area for the throw. Fourth, the receiver can break upfield then quickly come back to receive a short pass. (See Figure 19.)

When throwing a ball in, it must:

1) be thrown with both hands evenly in one continuous motion;

Figure 19
THROW-IN PLAYS

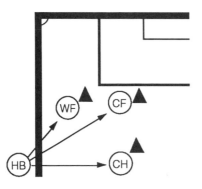

If someone is open, always throw to that person

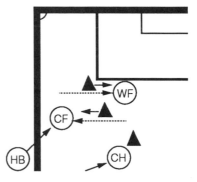

Wing creates open space, going to middle; striker switches to wing area for throw

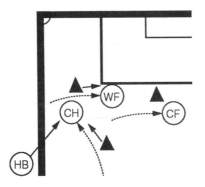

Wing vacates, creating space, center-half moves up for throw

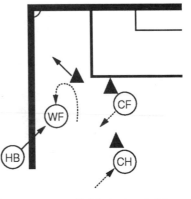

Winger runs upfield, but quickly comes back for throw

2) be delivered from behind and over the head;

3) be thrown straight, in front of the head, no twisting off to one side.

Furthermore,

4) the hands must follow through without the ball; it can't be just dropped to the ground;

5) both feet must be touching the ground as the ball is released;

6) the ball must land on the playing field, otherwise it is thrown again; and

7) it must touch another player before the thrower may touch it again.

The penalty for violating these rules, most often occurring when the back foot is raised too soon, is loss of possession. It's quite surprising how often violations occur for this relatively simple play. Upon violation the opposing team then gets to throw it in from the same spot. (See Figure 20.)

The key to throw-ins is quickness. The nearest person to the ball should scurry after it, or look for the ball-boy, and quickly throw it in before the defense gets organized and covers or *marks* potential receivers. I've seen kids who can throw nearly to the goal, setting up nice scoring opportunities.

A good throw-in gets the ball directly to a teammate's foot, in the air, or on one bounce. If the space in front of the teammate is open, then one should throw it ahead and let the player run up to it.

Another key to throw-ins is strength and the ability to whip the upper half of the body to get distance and speed on the ball. Hold the sides of the ball with the fingers spread apart and behind the ball. If a player can throw only a short distance, there is much less that can be done. Practice is, again, important. Have your child throw to you, and slowly, over time, add distance between you. I used to have my teams practice throwing a basketball, since it weighs more. I've even heard of a medicine ball being used. The idea is to arch the back and whip the ball, using the legs, back, and arms. Feet can be together, one in front of the other, or stepping forward. However, stepping forward, which generates more power, also leads to lifting the foot. The standing throw avoids this problem.

Figure 20
THROW-INS

Throw with both hands evenly

Ball delivered from behind and over head

Throw straight, hands must follow through without the ball

Hold sides of ball with fingers spread apart

Figure 20 (cont.)
THROW-INS

The most common mistake is to lift the back foot

Another common foul is to twist with the throw

Release from over the head, don't just drop the ball

Throw with both hands evenly from overhead, not to the side

Lifting the back foot is the cause of *many* penalties. It's a natural tendency to lift the foot *as* the ball is thrown. On a running throw the body's forward movement tends to pull the foot up, and the player should practice dragging the back toe to keep it down.

Finally, after the throw, the thrower should quickly get back on the field of play and move into position to receive a pass back from the target or do whatever is indicated by the circumstances.

CORNER KICKS

Perhaps the most underrated play in American soccer is the corner kick. Yet it is a play which allows for a free kick, placing the ball near the opponents' goal, with a whole group of teammates on the spot! This is an ideal scoring opportunity! Corner kicks occur often, and goals are often scored during corner kicks.

Corner kicks are awarded when the ball goes out of bounds, crossing the goal line, not the sideline, and a defensive player touched it last. The referee will point towards the corner of the field indicating a corner kick will be taken. A player, usually the forward wing, will place the ball at the corner of the field and kick it, trying to land it directly in front of the goal. The corner kicker may not kick the ball to himself. At younger ages the kid with the strongest foot will often take all corner and free kicks.

The typical strategy is to line up a wall of teammates outside of the penalty area, and have them charge the goal as the ball is kicked. The players then endeavor to score, usually by heading the ball into the net. I like to see six players involved. One stands in the opposite wing to get the ball if it passes the goal untouched, one goes up to the corner kicker for a possible short pass, and three tall players charge the goal from the eighteen yard line near the far post, angling towards the goal, looking to head or kick the ball in. Keep in mind that the offsides rule is in effect as soon as a player touches the ball. Another player or two remains outside the eighteen yard line to get the ball if it squirts out. (See Figure 21.)

As mentioned, often youth teams will have a big player who can kick the farthest come up and take the corner kick. If the ball drops in front of the goal, the chances to score are greatly increased. The object is to "power kick" the ball, and the kicking technique is: 1) for the right-footed kicker, lean a bit to the left of

Figure 21
CORNER KICKS

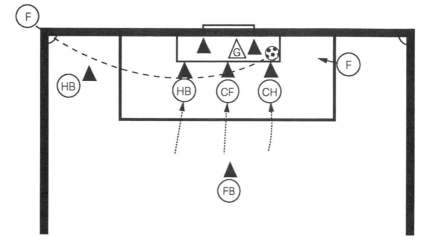

Halfback up for possible short pass, forward on other side if ball gets through, three players crash in from the eighteen for a shot

Lean left for full extension, lock ankles and explode into the ball

Hinge forward from waist for power and follow through

the ball to allow more kicking foot extension; 2) reach back farther with the kicking foot; 3) curl toes and lock ankles firmly; 4) explode into the ball with foot speed; and 5) follow through.

If the wind is strong into the goal, then the kick should place the ball right in front of the cross bar, attempting to score with the kick. Otherwise, the idea is to meet a teammate about six yards in front of the goal at head height.

At young ages, or if the wind is in the corner kicker's face, a teammate can quickly run towards the corner kicker and get a short pass. That player can then center the ball to the front of the goal, or give it back to the corner kicker for a center pass. Again, watch for offsides. It occurs often on corner kicks.

HEADING

Unfortunately, heading is usually one of the last skills learned by children. They do not practice the skill, for obvious reasons. It can hurt, giving a slight headache or sore neck if improperly done. However, there is a way to avoid this problem.

Soccer balls usually come in two main sizes, five and four. Size four is generally used prior to about twelve years of age. I recommend using the smaller ball for heading practice at any age for beginners. Also, it makes sense to let a *little* (not too much!) air out of the ball, soften it up a bit. I've even used a volleyball for heading practice since it's much lighter than a soccer ball. Toss the ball lightly to your child to build strength and confidence slowly. A good drill is to have your child kneel down to practice and thereby learn not to jump or lunge at the ball.

The keys to heading are concentration, keeping the eyes open and looking right at the point of the ball where contact will be made, making the neck rigid, and then making contact with the top of the forehead. Both feet should be on the ground if possible and the body should be balanced. Hands can make a fist.

Often kids will cringe, close their eyes, and let the ball land on top of the head. That's not only terrible mechanics, providing no control of where the ball goes, it also hurts. The upper forehead, just below the curve, is the strongest part of the head. It allows for continued eye contact and control and placement of the ball.

The player must know what to do with the ball *before* it arrives. Then it's just a matter of execution. One option is to retract the head and drop the ball to the ground for ground play. This is all right if defenders are not too close. The second option is to pass it from the head. This requires a choice of where to strike the ball to send it in the desired direction, and how hard to strike to get the desired distance. By simply turning the head a bit, the direction of the ball can be changed. Practice is needed here! Head and shoulders alone are used for short passes. For longer passes, the legs, in a boxer position, should be used to assist in giving strength and distance to the headed ball. This technique is to get under the ball, arch the back, tense the upper body, draw in the chin, and then thrust the head through the ball. Don't just let the ball hit the head, take command of it! (See Figure 22.)

Often it is necessary to leave the ground, to get "up" on the ball and be able to strike it on the side. This also occurs when another player is also trying to head the ball. Avoid lunging at the ball, jump straight up, hinge at the waist, and swing the legs forward upon contact.

Heading is very often done in front of the goal, from centering passes or corner kicks, in an attempt to score or to defend. Many, many goals are scored by heading. Try to head the ball very hard, and aim downward to make the goalie's job more difficult.

Heading is also used often against punts and goal kicks when the ball is high in the air. Since the ball travels a long distance before it is headed, it has the greatest potential to hurt. I recommend your child not undertake to head such balls until he has had sufficient experience and practice, and until his neck is more muscularly developed. Coaches may urge kids to do it, but if you are not sure your child is strong enough, tell him to forget it. You will each know when to undertake heading such balls.

TACKLING

This skill is risky business. I usually teach the kids that good defense means not having to tackle the ball. By definition, a tackle is an attempt to remove the ball from another player. In Chapter 8, we teach that defense should usually be passive, falling back, slowing down the ball. The primary principle of defense is never to

Figure 22
HEADING

Toss lightly to your child's forehead

Eyes on ball, neck rigid, body balanced, in a boxer position

Practice on the knees to learn to avoid lunging

Don't cringe or close eyes and let ball land on top of head

Figure 22 (cont.)
HEADING

Turning the head can change direction

Jump straight up, hinge at waist, thrust head forward

Dive heading can be effective but make sure no one is near

High balls require a strong neck

Figure 23
SLIDE TACKLING

A risky play to be used as a last ditch to stop the ball, also leads to injuries. Must touch ball first and not cause danger

let the ball be dribbled by you. In tackling, this chance is taken. If one fails, the ball gets by and the offense gets a higher percentage attack because the tackler is now out of the play.

There are times when tackling has a better chance, such as when the dribbler goes down the sideline and can be hemmed in, when a player is double teamed, or when another defender is covering the area.

Timing is important. It's good to feint a tackle and then charge when the ball is dribbled out. Another good time to tackle is just *as* the player receives the ball and does not yet have it under control. A shoulder charge is permissible, just keep the arms in and don't shove. The shoulder is used to stop forward progress, and the inside of the foot is planted firmly in front of the ball.

A slide tackle is a dangerous desperation play. It's dangerous because missing the ball may lead to a penalty. Also, the tackler is now on the ground, clearly out of the play, even if successful. Like everything else, there is a time for it, especially when a striker is going at the goal and the tackle is the only hope. The technique for a slide tackle is quite similar to the slide in baseball. One leg is tucked in for cushion, hands raised to avoid injury. Don't slide from behind the opponent or a free kick and penalty card will quickly be called. (See Figure 23.)

SHOOTING

The team needs someone who wants the net, who thinks about it constantly. Beyond desire, accuracy of the shot is the most important talent. It comes from shooting the ball thousands of times from all angles. Juggling and passing skills and drills are very helpful; but shooting the ball under pressure, with a goalie, is the best practice. If your child is a striker, get a goalie and defender (your spouse and you), and let the child shoot until exhausted.

The upper corners of the net are the best targets, the lower corners next best. The far post is usually the best, because shots are harder to stop, and leave a chance for another shot if they go wide. Ground shots are the toughest for the goalie to catch.

From a distance get power from the instep. Curl the toes so the foot is like a fist. Don't strike it too low. Many shots sail high over the crossbar for this reason. As with any hard pass, the head *must* stay down and still.

Usually there is little time to settle the ball, so a one-touch volley is needed. These must be practiced. Concentration on the point of contact, dead center on the side of the ball, is needed. Take it out of the air or on a hop. Always think about the net.

A parent can stand at the side of the penalty area and serve centering passes to a striker. Even if there are just the two of you, it's *very* good practice. You don't need a net, just a wall of some kind will do. (See Figure 24.)

Figure 24
SHOOTING

Feed to your child some one-touch volleys to shoot

Shooting gallery

7.

FIELD POSITIONS

One of the first questions a parent will have is, "What position should my child play?" Eleven players on each team take the field. Various formations can be employed, and these are discussed in the next chapter. Different positions sometimes have different names depending on the league, club, or even coach's preference.

The players who play up forward, attacking the other team's goal and trying to score, are called just that, *forwards*. If they generally play on the right side they are *right forward,* or *right wing*. It is the same for the left side. The forward player in the middle of the field is the *center forward*. If there are two inside forwards, then the one to the left is called the *inside left forward*, playing just inside the left wing. It is the same for the *inside right forward*. Forwards are also called *strikers*, although I've often heard this term reserved for the center forward.

The players who play back by their own goal, defending it, are called *backs* or *fullbacks*. On the right side it's *right fullback,* and on the left it's *left fullback*. These fullbacks are sometimes called *wing backs*. The one in the center is called the *center fullback* or *stopper*. Sometimes there is another defensive player who is even farther back than the center fullback and is called the *sweeper*.

A third group or rank of players are in between the forwards and fullbacks, and they are called, not surprisingly, *halfbacks*. There are *right, left (wing halves)*, and *center halfbacks*.

Last, but certainly not least, not by a long shot, is the *goalie*, also known as the *keeper*.

There are some guidelines coaches use initially to determine where players should be positioned. Parents can also use these to guide their children initially, although it's preferable to prepare your children to play multiple positions in their first few years. The main rules of thumb are that the wings have speed and ability to dribble with speed. The center forward has speed, good skills, aggressiveness, and a desire to score. Halfbacks are endurance runners and usually have the best skills, and the center halfback also needs leadership and game savvy. The fullbacks are big and strong, good headers, defensive-minded players, and the stopper is aggressive and fearless. The goal keeper is often a superb overall athlete, with excellent hands, preferably tall with long arms, and much courage. Left-footed people play on the left side, or at least those with the strongest left feet; vice versa on the right side. Those who play up the middle need to be able to use both feet effectively.

That's a good initial description of what's needed at each position, and your child will fit one of these categories. The nice thing about soccer is that it accommodates all sizes, speeds, and abilities. However, the bottom line is what happens on the field, and that is where positions are earned.

We'll talk a lot more in Chapter 7 about field dynamics for each position. Initially, it's important that children understand the areas of the field they are responsible for, and not just roam indiscriminately all over the place. Eventually they will learn they may leave the area, and engage in plays such as *overlap* or *switch* (discussed later). However, forwards generally stay in the front half, fullbacks in the back half; left side positions stay left of the middle of the field and vice versa for the right side. Midfielders play between the penalty areas. (See Figure 25.)

FORWARDS

Forwards are offensive players. Their main job is to score or to assist in scoring. As stated earlier, they must have speed to be able to break away from defenders and execute a strike on goal. Forwards must be able to dribble. I remember a young girl named Stacey with great speed, whose coach played her at fullback. I could see she was frustrated with the position, bottled up. She needed to play up front where she could run freely. Eventually she

Figure 25
SOCCER FIELD POSITIONS

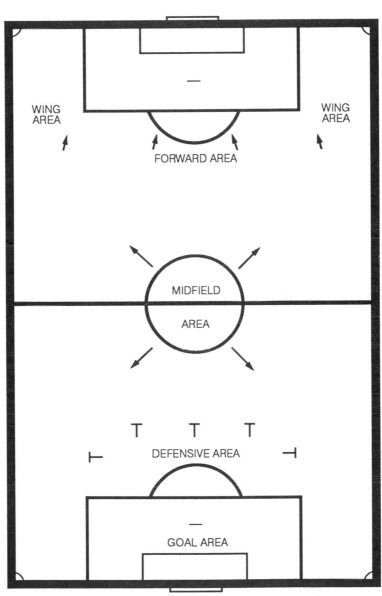

Forwards generally stay in forward half of the field, fullbacks are responsible for the defensive area, and halfbacks play between the two eighteen yardlines. Side players cover their side

quit the team, although she could have been a great player if the coach had positioned her properly.

The primary scoring strategy is for the wing forward on either side to dribble the ball down the sideline and get as close to the endline as possible. Then he "centers" the ball, that is, passes it towards the front of the goal to the striker for a shot. The reason we need to attack from the wing is that the forwards on offense generally cannot advance farther than the ball. See the "offside" rule in Chapter 8 for more detail. This rule essentially means that offensive progress needs to be *earned with the ball*. The purpose of the rule is to prevent players from just hanging out in front of the other team's goal. Specifically, it states that a player can't be further forward than the ball, when it is played, unless the goalie *and another defender* are between him and the goal. So if the wing moves the ball up towards the corner, other forwards and the striker can also advance, keeping even with the ball, to the front of the goal area.

Another reason we strike from the wing is that it's much easier to advance the ball along the sideline than up the middle where defenders are more numerous and can approach from any angle. It's just easier to attack along the wing, so that's why it's done. (See Figure 26.)

This means that wing forwards need two strong skills. First, they need to be able to speed dribble, to outrun a defending fullback into the wing corner of the field. Second, while on a dead run, they need to be able to execute a centering pass to the middle for the striker. While all basic skills are needed, speed dribbling and the center pass on the run are essential. I had a girl once with good speed, who could get the ball into the corner, but she could not *finish*, that is, execute the center pass. *Both* skills are needed!

For players in this position, these two skills should be practiced above all others. A speed dribbling drill was mentioned in the chapter on dribbling; just finish it with a centering pass each time. The trick is to plant the inside foot and, with a slight twist towards the middle, *very quickly* come around with the passing foot striking the side of the ball with the instep above the big toe. Repetition is the key; do it a dozen times each practice. Perfect the skill! Your child, as a wing forward, should start with the ball at mid-field, speed dribble down the sideline, and then pass the ball to the front of the goal. You can run down the middle, as if you were a center

Figure 26
ATTACK FROM THE WING

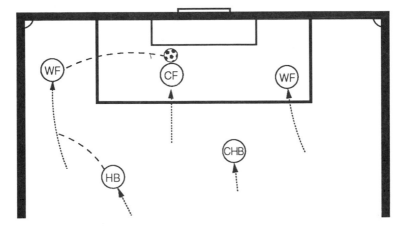

Ball is passed up to the wing forward who then advances it to the corner and centers it to a striker for the shot

Center pass on the run: plant foot points to center, quick kicking action, strike ball with area by big toe

forward, to provide a moving target.

You can also practice defending against your child to provide some pressure. Young wing forwards need to learn how to fake and feint and give themselves a window for the centering pass. Not much is needed, only a split second and enough space to get the ball by the defender.

Wings are sprinters: they should condition themselves with many wind sprints, about thirty yards each. It's essential to properly stretch before doing wind sprints. Also, encourage your child to develop the left foot. Any child who can execute a left-footed center pass will receive more playing time, because American players tend to develop only the right foot. Left-footed players are always valuable and will receive more playing time.

Wings score plenty of goals. When breaking towards the corner they often can get away from the defender and strike directly on goal. They can shoot the ball from their wing position if in scoring range. I always tell them to aim for the far goal post. This is because goalies usually cheat to the inside or near post, and also because if a far post shot is wide there is still a chance for another forward to recover it. Wings also head goals on corner kicks and jump on loose balls shot from the opposite wing. As a wing, your child should be encouraged to practice shots from the corner of the penalty area.

Wings should generally stay as wide, as close to the sideline, as they can. Don't bunch into the middle of the field. It's the half-back's job to get the ball up and out to the wing for an attack down the sidelines. If the ball is passed up to the wing corner, the wing had better be there to get it. Often the pass will be a long or crossing kick into the wing corner. The wing forward needs to be in position to sprint to the ball, advance it, and execute the centering pass. That's why speed is necessary; it becomes a foot race.

Wings need to practice corner kicks and heading goals. They don't usually need to do throw-ins, since they are usually the players receiving them. Wings should practice receiving throw-ins, and this is something a parent can help with. Throw a dozen or so balls at your child, from as far away as you can. Mix them up. Your child will receive, and so needs to learn to control, many bad throws.

Center forwards are among the chosen people of soccer. They

have it all—speed, ball control skills, and aggressiveness. Some height would be nice for heading, but the essential ingredient is a knack for the net. In every group of kids, there is always at least one who really wants the net, wants to score. Sure, all kids like to score. I'm talking about the one who is always looking to put the ball into the net and who can get it there! The *desire* is essential. How often do you see players with the ball in front of the goal, and they don't shoot? The striker must be constantly thinking of the net, of scoring. The player who produces goals will get to shoot, it's as simple as that. It's often not the best player, or the most skilled. It's often someone who thinks more about the net than anyone else; it's in the blood.

Strikers need to develop shooting skills. So this is what they spend most of their time practicing. Stand your striker on the eighteen yard line, to receive your passes endlessly from both sides of the field. Have someone stand in goal so your child can get used to shooting *around* the goalie. Young players also need to practice scoring with just one touch. In a game there is often no time to settle the ball; just focus on the point of contact and shoot, shoot, shoot. Practice with both feet! A good drill is to put five or six forwards in the penalty area and keep throwing balls into their midst. The kid who gets the ball, shoots. Everyone else is to prevent the person with the ball from shooting. As soon as a shot is taken, throw in another ball. The winner is the one with the most goals.

Strikers need to be good in one-on-one situations, since this is what they constantly are faced with. Practice here will pay off in goals! The best strikers can score on a breakaway, and such situations must also be practiced.

FULLBACKS

Fullbacks are defensive players. Their job is to stop goals. When a goal is scored, it's not the goalie's fault. It's usually the defense's fault. The soccer goal is pretty big; fullbacks must stop players from getting close enough to take good shots.

Wing fullbacks on the right and left side have the primary job of *containing* the wing forwards. As we said earlier, the wing's job is to penetrate to the corners and center the ball. The wing full back's job is to slow that penetration and stop the center pass. Fullbacks must stay between the ball and the goal, move with the fakes and feints, and look for an opportunity to get a foot on the ball. If they take a risk and miss, the chance for a score radically increases. They must be cautious, conservative, and alert.

We'll talk in depth later about defensive strategy. The key is to hold ground. Most kids make the very bad mistake of overcharging the ball. *It happens all the time.* An offensive player with even minimum skills will see this and simply sweep the ball around a charging defender. There are times to attack, especially if you have backups, and there are techniques to help tackle the ball. More times than not, though, a charge will fail. When it does, the offensive player will penetrate and the charging defensive player is out of the action. So the idea is to hold ground, prevent or delay penetration, keep the dribbler wide along the sideline, wait for help, and seek good percentage opportunities to tackle the ball. (See Figure 27.) But remember, when a forward penetrates behind the fullback, there is no one left but the goalie, and that is trouble! Talk to your child about this concept!

A fullback must know the location of any forward in the area and anticipate that the other team will try to play the ball to the wing. Good anticipation will often be rewarded with a stolen ball. When a halfback with the ball glances at the wing forward, odds are a pass will follow. So, the fullback anticipates this and breaks to a point between them to intercept a pass, or breaks into the corner to intercept a long pass.

Wing fullbacks need to be able to do throw-ins and should practice them.

When the ball is on the other side of the field, the wing fullback must protect the area in front of the goal. He anticipates the center pass, and makes sure the center fullback marks the striker. He looks for other forwards trying to sneak around through the "back door," behind the defense. All players in front of the goal must be marked one-on-one by a defender.

The center fullback and sweeper are the last line of defense. They must never let the ball get behind them. They must always know which players are in front of the goal and must "mark" or defend these players closely. They do not leave the area unless another defender is there to back them up. Communication is

Figure 27
PLAYING FULLBACK

One of the most important concepts in soccer is to hold ground, delay the ball, force or pressure mistakes, and above all don't overcommit

constant and essential. They must listen for instructions from the goalie, who has a broader field of vision.

Of course, once a fullback has the ball he tries to move it safely up the field. *Never, never, never,* pass the ball towards the front of your own goal. This is the cardinal rule of defense. Defenders must pass upfield, towards the sideline. If the area in front of them is open, they *may* dribble forward, as far as possible. Others will fill in behind.

Center fullbacks are usually tough kids. They need to be very aggressive, absolutely determined to keep the ball away from the goal. When the ball is in the penalty area, they *must* get to it, and must, if under pressure, kick it away as far as possible. They must be willing to take a last ditch slide tackle. They *rarely* dribble the ball or take any chances in front of the goal. Their job is to get the ball away from the goal. Obviously, they don't want to give it up and should endeavor to pass it safely to a halfback or even back to the goalie. The highest priority is to *clear* it away. Their best weapon is often a powerful *clearing* kick which sends the ball a long distance, if needed, in *any* direction.

I once coached a girl named Lauren who was a natural defender. She had the knack for being in the right place when needed, always anticipating the play. She was not tall, but strong and fearless, and she scooped up and cleared free balls with aggressiveness.

Center fullbacks must be able to head the ball away from the goal. They must take on any offensive player and beat that person to the ball without fouling or obstructing. If they do, particularly in the penalty area, the price can be very high—a penalty kick and most likely a goal.

As defensive quarterbacks, center fullbacks always look for the offsides and can call offsides traps (discussed later). If the goalie gets caught out of goal or falls down, it is the center fullback who must go to the goal-mouth and try to deflect any shots, without using the hands.

HALFBACKS

Halfbacks don't need size or great speed, but they are usually the most skilled and consistent players on the team. The center of the field sees the most action; that's where the ball is most often. The ball comes from every possible direction and height. When halfbacks have the ball, defenders come to them from all angles. They must be able to control the ball under great pressure. They are the long distance runners of soccer and must *nearly always* be running. Halfbacks are also called *midfielders* or *linkmen*.

My experience is that soccer games are won and lost at midfield. If the midfielders, the halfbacks, cannot control the ball, it will wind up back by their fullbacks. The team that can keep the ball in front of the other team's goal the longest time will score. It's a game of percentages.

So it's the job of midfielders to prevent the ball from penetrating through to their defense. They must control it and move it up to their offense. This is what wins soccer games.

Halfbacks don't need speed. It's good to have but not essential; their job is to control and pass the ball. They also need quickness; quick footwork, fakes, feints, whatever it takes to control the ball and advance it to a forward.

A typical routine for a halfback is to receive a pass from a defender, shield the ball, put a "move" on and get enough time to pass the ball forward. This is called the "transition," where they start by facing their own defense, receive a pass, and turn to play the ball up to their offense.

A nice transition move for halfbacks receiving a pass from a fullback is called the *halfturn*. I learned it from some visiting British coaches. The player, facing the backfield, wants to receive the pass, not slow the ball down too much, turn and pivot with the ball under control, and then advance it upfield. The idea is to trap the ball *while turning on the other foot*. The foot receiving the ball touches it only gently, slowing it down just enough to have it under proper control, and then guides it out in front, ready to advance upfield. (See Figure 28.)

Halfbacks do most of the throw-ins. This is because the wings need to be free to receive the pass, and the fullbacks need to defend if the pass is intercepted. Halfbacks more than anyone else need to practice this skill. An effective throw-in is a valuable offensive weapon particularly when near the offensive goal. There it can be similar in value to a corner kick.

The center halfback is the team's quarterback, the leader, often the most skilled player on the team, and the one who directs the offense by constantly calling out plays and directions. This player has the ability to "see" the whole field. The center of the field is where the ball usually is; it crosses this area all game long. The center halfback must control it, and get it up to one of the wings. The center halfback is also often a second striker, tracking the forwards and picking up loose balls and rebounds for shots on goal. This position requires the ability to shoot from a distance.

My daughter played this position, and she had an uncanny ability to see the open players and pass the ball perfectly to their feet. This is what midfielders must be able to do.

The center halfback helps out the wing-halfbacks when they are in trouble, calling for them to "square," e.g. pass the ball laterally to them. She then initiates the offense, generally dribbling if possible, then getting the ball up to one of the wings. A key play for all players, and particularly the center halfback, is the "give and go" (discussed later). Usually a halfback will give it to the center

Figure 28
TURNING WITH THE BALL

Begin to pivot on plant foot, farthest from the ball, as the ball approaches

While turning, touch ball enough to slow and control it

As ball proceeds upfield, complete turn and dribble

Figure 29
GOALIE POSITIONING

Crouched, weight forward, hands up over knees

Upon a shot, hands form a "W"

Legs together on low shots

Get in front of the ball and use the body when possible

halfback who will quickly return it to the same halfback who is then sprinting upfield. This also works with the striker, who dishes it back to the center halfback and then moves into a forward gap.

The center halfback needs to be able to head the ball, and this skill should be practiced. These players also receive many throw-ins and should work with the halfbacks on different routines.

GOALIE

Last but not least! The goalie must be a top athlete. In European soccer play, the goalie is often the best athlete on the team. This player doesn't need great foot skills, but does need to be super quick, have excellent hands, be smart, courageous, able to punt a long distance, and be very, very tough.

Goalies position themselves between the ball and the center of the goal, usually a few yards out from the goal line, never *in* the goal standing on the goal line. Yet the goalie doesn't want to be so far out from the goal line that a high shot can get over his or her hands and still go under the cross bar. The goalie stance is a crouched position, hands forward over the knees, weight on the front of the feet, eyes on the ball, ready to spring sideways into the path of the shot. (See Figure 29.) It's important to watch the ball at all times in flight, right into the hands. The hands are close together when catching a shot, thumbs touching in a figure "W", fingers spread apart.

If at all possible, the goalie should use the body to back up the hands, get in front of the ball. If the shot is low, the legs should be together.

For shots to the side of the keeper, goalies must hurl themselves laterally towards the ball, in a horizontal position. (See Figure 30.) The concept behind the horizontal position is that it allows both hands *equal play*, since relative to the body they are centered. If the player merely reaches to the side, the hands are not equally balanced. Soccer balls are shot *very hard*, and both hands are needed to catch the ball. Horizontal dives allow both hands to be equally and comfortably engaged in catching the ball. To stop a hard, direct shot, the goalie can hop back a step to cushion the ball. Watch the ball all the way to the stomach and pull it in.

Figure 30
GIVE BOTH HANDS EQUAL PLAY

Face down dive forces left hand to do all the work, right hand is ineffective *With body turned more outward, both hands can be involved*

I used to lay a mattress out on the field for my son, and he would dive for the ball, landing on the mattress. After a while I put a small mat, and eventually he knew how to fall. Another good drill was to let him kneel on the ground and I would throw the ball to either side of him. He hit the ground much more softly and learned how to break the fall with hip, elbow, and upper back.

Ground shots are the toughest. A goalie must try to get behind the ball, legs together, knees straight, and scoop the ball up with the hands close together, palms out. Ground shots to the side are caught after diving and lying on the ground, blocking the ball with the body. Goalies also need to know how to "time" high shots. Many goals are scored this way in youth soccer.

Your local high school may have a soccer wall with the goal post area painted on it. These large wooden walls are often used for shooting practice. I made a lot of use of ours for goalie practice with my son. It's good for two people because the ball comes right back to you, and it saves a great deal of time.

Figure 31
HIGH SHOTS ON GOAL

Always catch the ball if at all possible

But punch or tip it over the crossbar if needed on a very hard shot

I would shoot, and Joe would try to stop it. I would shoot long high shots, so he could begin to judge his timing when to jump for the ball and to know how far out of the net he could safely come. On high hard shots, for anything high enough to require the arms to be fully stretched upwards, the goalie should learn how to tip the ball up above the crossbar. (See Figure 31.) It gives the other team a corner kick, but it's better than a goal. The keeper needs to learn what he or she can catch, and what needs to be deflected. Always catch a ball if possible, but tip it if needed. Punch the ball if it's necessary, particularly if the player is in a crowd and it's tough to get both hands on it. A goalie can also kick a ball if needed, but catching is *by far* the preferable action. A hard shot is tough to catch with outstretched hands. A good catching drill for goalies is to throw a small medicine ball back and forth. This also strengthens the hands and wrists.

Occasionally, an opponent will break away from the fullback and come upon the goalie one-on-one. If this happens, and if there

Figure 32
CHARGING THE STRIKER

Only when no other defender can assist, the goalie charges, forcing a wide shot

Stay balanced, on the feet, arms out, anticipate the shot

is no chance for a fullback to intervene, then the goalie must charge the opponent. We don't want to charge too soon, allowing the opponent to loft a soft shot over the goalie's head, or pass to a teammate. As soon as the ball enters the penalty area, the charge is on. The goalie charges, arms outstretched, legs balanced, eyes on the ball and on the opponent's legs, anticipating the contact with the ball. Sometimes the forward will dribble the ball too far out in front and the goalie will be able to dive on it (dangerous) or tackle it (safer). The goalie must try to *time* the dribbles and charge as the ball is swept forward, particularly if it is dribbled out too far from the attacker.

In any event, the idea behind charging is to put pressure on the striker, obstruct that player's vision of the goal, and force an early shot. As the goalie charges, the available shooting lanes and angles become narrower, and it's *much* tougher to score. Often the shot will be wide, or deflect off the goalie. It's essential to stay on the feet and be able to react to the loose ball. (See Figure 32.) It's useful to get a very long clothesline, attach the ends to each post, and have someone stretch it to various distances so the goalie can become familiar with the angles and a striker's available shooting lanes. It drives the concept home.

When the ball is in the opponent's half of the field, the goalie should stay up by the eighteen yard line, or even farther if he is fast enough. Sometimes a long pass from an opponent will go farther than expected, and the goalie can easily get to the ball. This should be done only in rare instances, because one slip and the opponent will have an open net. It happened once to me as I played goalie in a pick-up game. It was a most frustrating feeling to watch as the ball was taken to the net, well out of my reach.

As players advance onto the goalie's side of the field, the goalie slides back, always on a line between the ball and the center of the goal. Naturally, in the thick of action, the goalie is only several feet from the goal line.

One of the goalie's main jobs is to look for opponents who have no defender "marking" them. The goalie identifies the player, usually by number, calling for defenders to mark the player. Keepers should not be afraid to shout to other teammates about what's going on; they have the best view of the whole area.

Upon a shot, often a long high shot—usually on direct kicks or corner kicks—if the goalie can get to the ball he or she will shout out "keeper!". This instructs her teammates to get out of the way and let the goalie catch the ball. Do not say, "I've got it," since that is considered confusing and is a violation.

The toughest job for a goalie is to dive on a loose ball. I've always believed, particularly at youth levels where the kids *swarm* in front of the goal, that goalies should have forearm guards and hard hats. Referees *are* usually pretty quick to stop play. Still, too often, a player will try to kick the ball out of a goalie's hands and this leads to injuries. I think the rules need to do a much better job of protecting goalies at youth levels, and I welcome the recent allowance by the Federation Internationale de Futbol Association (F.I.F.A.) of headgear.

The goalie must always know who is in the penalty area. The main offensive strategy is to get a centering pass in front of the goal, and strikers always look then to head the ball into the net. The goalie must anticipate this, and snatch the ball away or block the head shot. It's often hard to judge when to run out to catch a high pass and when to stay and defend the shot. With practice, the goalie will know what he can do and what he can expect out of his defense. A good rule of thumb is that if the ball is in the goal box, get to it; if outside of the six yard line, be cautious. However, it's *always* easier to catch a high pass than defend a hard shot. So tell your child to get the ball whenever possible.

Goalies need to be able to punt and throw the ball long distances. The throw involves curling the ball in the hand and slinging it underhand in bowling fashion, sidearm, or overhead, as needed. Usually a throw or punt to the opposite side of the field from which the ball came will find less of a crowd and should be the first choice looked at. Find someone alone to pass to. Don't rush it! (See Figure 33.)

Punting is more difficult. However, if nearby teammates are marked, a punt is the best option. The basics of punting are:

1) Face the location or player you want to punt to and gauge the wind.

2) Bend forward, holding the ball in the palm of the left hand (for a right-footed kick), cradling or guiding it gently with the right hand.

3) Still bending, with head down take two quick steps—a short step with the right foot and a larger leaping step with the left foot. Remember, only four steps are allowed the goalie.

4) Holding the ball low, still bending forward, and facing slightly to the right of the target, softly lob the ball to the place where the kicking foot will meet it. Don't throw it too high, let it travel in the air as short a distance as possible. However, do *lob it forward* to allow for full forward body movement.

5) Lock the kicking foot, and strike the ball hard and explosively with the instep, right on the shoelaces. *Leg speed is essential.* Look at the point of the ball, underside about one-fourth of the way up from the bottom, where contact will be made.

6) Follow through fully and gracefully; the body will pull the plant foot forward into a hop.

7) Practice, practice, practice.

The goalie should usually first look to throw the ball to a teammate who is free. Kicking away leads to lost possession a higher percentage of the time. However, at younger ages, kids can kick a *lot* farther than they can throw. Often the coach will just

Figure 33
PUNTING OR THROWING BALL INTO PLAY

Point plant foot at target, bend forward, take two steps

Head down, leap to plant foot, lob ball to point of contact

Lock ankle, explode into ball with foot speed and follow through

Sling ball to open player

want to get the ball as far away from the goal as possible, particularly when the fullbacks have trouble receiving a goalie pass and controlling the ball. Again, game dynamics depend on the skills of the players. If the team is not skilled, then the coach may choose just to have players kick the ball as far as possible and hope to get lucky. It happens a lot in American soccer, but not often in European soccer where kids learn soccer skills as soon as they can walk.

Goalies need to defend penalty kicks. Often the best defense is to unsettle the kicker. Take time, walk around, don't be in a hurry to get set up. Make the kicker wait. Stare him in the eye. As he goes for the ball, sway a bit to one side, opposite to the side you intend to protect. The first step should be out a bit and then drive to the side. Usually the ball travels low to the ground, so be ready to reach far and low.

8.

OFFENSE AND DEFENSE

TEAM STRATEGY AND GAME DYNAMICS

Most American youth teams seem to play three forwards, three halfbacks, three fullbacks, a sweeper, and a goalie. There are many variations on this, depending on the abilities of the players, game conditions, and the other team's approach.

Sometimes the "extra" player, the sweeper above, is a rover, and will roam freely behind the defense or "mark" an exceptional player on the opposing team.

Sometimes, particularly at older ages, teams will put the additional player up front and go with two inside strikers. Or the middle halfback will cheat forward a bit. I've seen lineups with five forwards. But usually American youth soccer goes with the additional defensive player, the rover/sweeper.

As to game strategy, soccer is less technical than American football where each play is carefully diagrammed and thought out in advance. Soccer is a fluid game, and players pretty much need to decide what to do in each individual situation. Of course, even football involves individual discretion, particularly when the "play" breaks down. However, soccer depends much more on the dynamics of the moment.

This is not to say that there are no "plays" in soccer, or an overall strategy. There clearly are both. However, soccer strategy involves more a system of *concepts* which are applied in given situations.

OFFENSIVE STRATEGY

Overlap: The Whole Field is Yours

Earlier we talked about field positions. Some people attack, some defend, some work at midfield transition. Many coaches will tell their players not to cross midfield if they are defenders, not to come back past midfield if they are forwards, that right halfbacks don't go on the left side of the field, and the like. "Play your position!" Well, your children have to do what they are told, and they do have the primary responsibility for their section of the field. But *overlap* is an essential part of soccer, and players need to be able to take advantage of opportunities to advance the ball.

The concept of overlap is that a player, with or without the ball, can move past a teammate in front, or to the side, if it creates a favorable offensive condition. If a player moves out of position, then other players need to adjust, to fill in, to rotate, and to make sure the defense remains strong. The overlapped player drops back, or another player comes over. The concept requires some experience. Players need to know how to fill in for each other and how to back each other up. This is why youth coaches worry about overlaps, because the kids aren't always experienced enough to back each other up. However, your children need to understand the concept, and to know that some day soon they will be expected to overlap, or even to change positions just to confuse the defense. (See Figure 34.)

Attack from the Wings

We have already discussed this concept in detail in the preceding chapters, particularly in Chapter 7 when discussing the wing position. The idea basically is to get the ball as far forward as possible, and it turns out that this is most easily done by getting it into the corners or wing areas. *You can never overstate this concept to your child!* An attack down the sidelines into the corner can only be defended from one side (the sideline being on the other side).

Figure 34
OVERLAP AND ROTATE

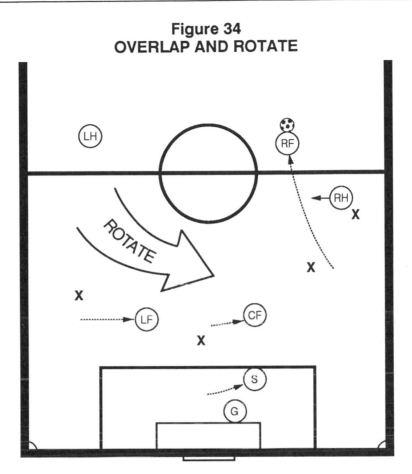

The right fullback (RF) sees an open field and dribbles the ball upfield. The other fullbacks and sweeper then rotate towards the undefended area, and the overlapped right halfback (RH) fills in also

There are more defenders in the middle, but a sideline attack usually involves only one defender, and therefore a one-on-one situation. Also, the offside rule means that offensive ground must be earned by the ball, so an approach to the corner allows the striker to advance in front of the goal in line with the ball.

In setting up a wing attack, the halfbacks or center forward must get the ball to a wing forward. An inside striker can do so as well. Usually it is best to pass the ball well ahead of the wing who can then run up to it, particularly if the wing area is free of defenders. This allows the wing forward to sprint past the defender, retrieve the ball, advance it, and then execute a centering pass to the striker. The pass to the wing depends on timing, and will improve with practice and experience. (See Chapter 7, Figure 26.)

The wing forward should move the ball as close to the goal line as possible before centering the ball out in front of the goal. If the defender can be beaten, the forward can angle towards the goal for a shot, or otherwise angle for the corner and plan the move that will set up a good centering pass. As stated earlier, the striker cannot penetrate further upfield than the ball because of the offside rule. Therefore, if the wing gets the ball near the goal line, the striker will be able to get directly in front of the goal to receive the center pass.

Give and Go

It's the best offensive play there is! It's so simple, and yet for some reason kids just don't do it. They pass the ball to a teammate (just getting them to pass takes time!), and then they stop! The moment of a pass is the best time to shake a defender. Often the defender is off balance looking at the passed ball, thinking about it, and wondering whether it can be gotten. Perhaps they just stop when the pass is made, figuring the job is done.

The trick is to take advantage of the defender's momentary pause. Pass the ball, and then *in the same motion* break upfield! Breaking forward in the same motion with the pass also helps the receiver to notice the breaking player. The receiver then passes the ball back. This is also called a *wall pass*, because the first receiver one-touches it back, like the ball rebounding off a wall. It's simple. *Give* the ball to a teammate, and *go* get the return pass. *It*

Figure 35
GIVE AND GO

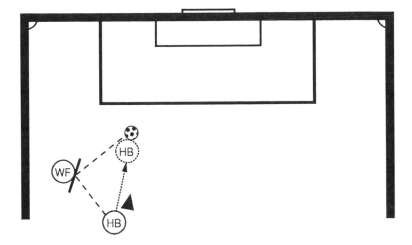

The give and go or wall pass—the halfback passes to wing forward and dashes upfield for the return pass

Figure 36
MOVING OFF THE BALL

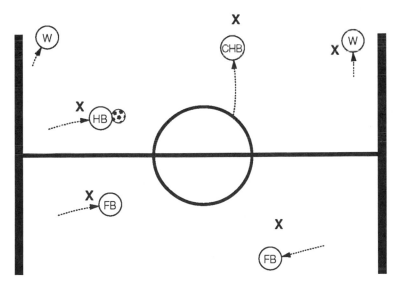

Halfback with ball moves away from defender (X). Fullback trails play in case HB loses ball. Center half sets up for a give and go. Wings move up for a corner pass. Everyone is involved in movement off ball

works most of the time, and I am just flabbergasted why we see so little of it. It's the bread-and-butter play of basketball, and it is so for one reason. *It works* a high percentage of the time! At older ages, where the game is more open, it is useful, but in youth soccer, a much closer game, it is an even more powerful play. Talk about this concept with your child, practice it. Let your young player kick the ball to you and then dash ahead for a return pass. The key is in breaking forward *as* one passes the ball; the receiver should notice it and quickly pass it back. (See Figure 35).

Safety Pass

Soccer is a game of ball control and ball possession. There may be no one upfield to safely receive a pass. Your child may not be able to safely dribble the ball because of approaching defenders. Maybe the player with the ball just doesn't think the defender can be beaten. If so, then pass the ball *back* to another teammate. It may seem like you are moving in the wrong direction; but remember, maintaining possession is the top priority of ball control. This play can also work as a give and go if the passer then breaks upfield to receive a return pass. Just don't pass the ball back near your own goal unless it's to the goalie.

Flow When Off the Ball

Sometimes the line between offense and defense is not clear. The concept of triangulation involves both offensive and defensive strategy. This is also called *giving support* to the ball carrier. It basically means that the people nearest a player with the ball form moving triangles so that one always has the option to pass forward, backward, or sideways as needed. For instance, if a player is facing or dribbling to the left of midfield, the forward player moves in the same direction, in position to receive a pass. The teammate behind moves likewise, and also defends the area left and to the rear in case the ball is tackled by a defender, or in case he is needed as an outlet. The concept is really quite simple, and it suggests only that teammates *flow with* the ball, giving good angles for a pass and staying close enough to receive a quick pass. (See Figure 36.)

Create or Move to Open Space

The concept of triangulation encourages each player to move to an open space, into an open position to receive a pass. However, the concept of creating open space is also universal. Players who do not have the ball must always decide where they are needed. They *never* just stand and watch, that's what fans are for. The concept of *moving off the ball* deals with what to do if you don't have the ball. Generally players move with the *flow* of the ball, upfield, downfield, right, or left. That's easy and natural. If near or upfield of the ball, players must create or move into open space, that is, get into position to receive the ball or create space for a teammate to receive a pass. The reason? Pretty obvious! Open space is a place where there are no defenders. It's open space! Now, of course, this is done so long as the teammate with the ball can get a pass off. There is no sense running to an open spot if the ball carrier can't see or reach the receiver. Players without the ball are also able to feint and fake, get their defender to lean one way so they can then dart the other way.

Often, plays are designed to *create* open space. This concept is an advanced one and requires maturity and experience. The *switch* play, discussed later, is one which creates open space. The idea is that a player creates an open space by *leaving* an area and taking a defender with him. This then allows a player to dribble or pass to that spot if another teammate is headed that way. I like this play best when a wing, halfback, and striker all switch positions. The wing drops back, halfback goes to striker, and striker goes to wing to receive a pass. The halfback goes to the goal to get the center pass. Open space will, if it works, be created both in the wing and at the center forward area. A typical way to make space, if for instance a halfback is dribbling the ball, would be for the wing forward to leave the space in front of the halfback. If the forward slides to midfield, taking his defender with him, then the dribbler has open space in front of him. (See Figure 37.)

Defenders will not likely be called upon to receive a pass, other than a possible safety pass. Their job is to back-up the player with the ball if on the same side of the field. In case it's stolen we need someone to be close by. A defensive teammate on the other side of the field must be positioned to defend against a possible breakaway if the ball is stolen. This is called *slanting*, and will be

Figure 37
CREATE OPEN SPACE

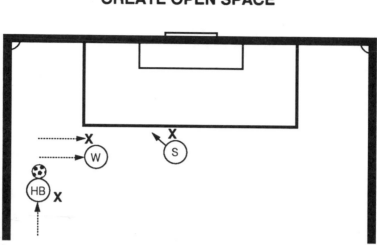

Not an easy concept for kids to apply. Here the wing moves towards the center of the field, taking defender (X) with her. The halfback with the ball is then free to dribble to the open space created by the wing's move. The striker then moves or angles for a center pass

Figure 38
WINGS STAY WIDE FOR CROSSING PASS

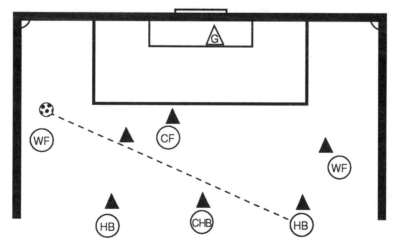

As defenders bunch towards the ball, a long crossing pass to the opposite wing can be a powerful play, catching the defense by surprise. This is why wings must stay wide

covered more when we talk about defensive strategy. It basically means the defender stays in the backfield well behind the ball.

Wings Stay Wide for Crossing Pass

As stated earlier, defensive players tend to flow with the ball, towards it. Therefore, a very effective offensive strategy is to boot the ball all the way across to the opposite side, catching defenders off balance and out of position.

This requires a pretty strong foot. It also requires that someone stay wide and away on the opposite side to receive such a pass. Often players on the opposite side of the field will tend to gravitate towards the center of the field. Wings can't allow this to happen. They must always stay wide. The "open space" will be towards the opposite sideline, and we need the wing forwards to always stay wide for any pass, from any angle, which will allow them to get the ball and penetrate into the corner. Staying wide also pulls a defender from the middle and opens up the area. (See Figure 38.)

Often, a player with the ball won't see that a wing is free for a crossing pass, and someone may need to help him. You will often hear someone yell out "cross," and that means that a wing is open across the field.

A crossing pass is a powerful offensive weapon. It catches defenders by surprise. Many "cheap" goals are scored off such situations. Of course, it requires a strong foot, so it is not seen often at younger ages.

Square

Once again, players are looking for people to pass to. As a general rule they will look upfield, along the sidelines, for a wing. Passing the ball into the center of the field is usually not the best thing to do, since that receiver can be attacked from any angle. It also sets up a good counterattack for the opponent if the ball is intercepted. We almost *never* pass the ball to the center of the field in front of our own goal. That's exactly where the opposition wants the ball, and it should never be done.

However, upfield, a pass into the center is occasionally the preferable option. This is so when the wings are covered and no other option exists. In this case, a midfielder, who is free, will yell out "square" which tells the player with the ball to pass it laterally

Figure 39
SQUARE

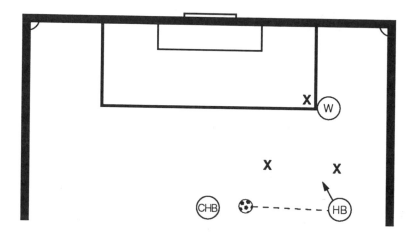

Here the halfback with the ball cannot advance, so the center half yells "square", thus calling for a lateral pass

to the center. The player with the ball may not have seen the teammate directly to one side. So it helps a lot to have someone yell it out. (See Figure 39.)

Switch

As stated at the beginning of this chapter, holding players to a single position on the field unnecessarily limits the possible offensive plays. For instance, if a wing is well covered, then how are we going to get the wing attack going? One way is to have the wing and striker *switch*. The wing heads into the midfield and the striker darts out towards the corner, in other words they *switch*. This play works best when the defenders are marking (defending) players very closely, instead of defending areas. It confuses the defense momentarily, allowing the striker time to get to the ball, advance it, and center the ball back to the wing or midfielder who is now striking to the goal.

Encourage Shots

Offense has to be a positive dynamic. Forwards and halfbacks should be encouraged to take shots. Yell out positive phrases like "Good try," "Keep shooting," or "Nice shot." Obviously, players need to learn to stay away from bad shots, as discussed in Chapter 4, but the general approach must be a positive one. They can't score if they don't shoot!

Run with the Ball

Often players get the ball and pass too quickly. If no defender is nearby, players must try to advance the ball. First, it gets the ball farther upfield; and second, it forces a defender to come to the ball, away from any potential receiver. If no one is pressuring, teammates should yell, "carry it," or "run with it." This tells the dribbler that no one is approaching from behind. When a defender does approach, yell out "man on," which signals that it's time to pass.

DEFENSIVE STRATEGY

As in many sports, defense is largely a matter of reaction. The offense sets the play into motion, and the defense needs to react and defend accordingly.

As mentioned in Chapter 7, most American youth teams will field three fullbacks and add a fourth defensive player as a sweeper or rover, or to key on an exceptional opposing player. Soccer is viewed worldwide largely as a defensive game. Scores are low because of this.

Pursuit

The first principle in good defense is pursuit. Someone has to go defend the person with the ball. Usually it's the nearest defender, the defender whose zone the ball enters. Sometimes it's a man-to-man defense. Whatever the case, someone *must* go after the dribbler. Often at youth levels we see a kid dribble a long way with no one pursuing. One hears coaches screaming, "Go to the ball!, go to the ball!"

Contain, Apply Pressure, But Don't Overcommit

The essence of soccer defense is *pressure*. We want to *slow down* and *contain* the offense, to *prohibit offensive players from getting past a defender with the ball,* and to pressure the ball carrier into making a mistake. Some people might think the main idea is to get the ball, and that is certainly one objective. However, the primary objective is to stay between the ball and the goal and apply pressure. This does not mean defenders should rush and attack the ball. How often do we see a player overcommit by rushing the ball, only to have the dribbler slip by? The best way to regain possession is to force a mistake, force a bad pass, and then get to the ball.

Defenders *must* learn to be patient, keep their feet balanced under them, and try to get the offensive player to commit first. I tell the kids to pretend they are going to charge, feint or fake a step, and then see if the dribbler commits. Sometimes just the presence of a defender will cause a player to kick the ball away and lose possession. The defender must block the dribbler's advance and then anticipate the next move. The defender should be close enough to apply pressure, but not so close that the dribbler can sweep by. The defender *must* stay balanced, weight forward on the balls of the feet. If the player with the ball hesitates long enough, then another defender may be able to provide support. When two defenders double team a player, the second defender to arrive tackles the ball or signals the other teammate to do so.

To summarize, the defender's job is to slow or stop forward progress of the player with the ball, apply pressure, and avoid going too quickly for the ball (unless the defender is sure he can get a foot on it). Obviously, a dribbler getting past a defender will penetrate closer to the goal and this requires another defender to assist (if there is another one between the ball and the goal). We covered tackling in Chapter 5, and this should be reviewed again.

Keep the Ball Away from the Middle

Similarly, if the ball is along the sideline, the defender's job is to ensure that the dribbler does not penetrate towards center field, particularly if near the goal. The defensive objective is to continue to force the player with the ball to stay wide, along the sidelines and also try to get in the way of any center pass. Once again, we are more concerned to keep the attacker away and under control, and to tackle the ball only when certain it will be successful.

Good offense tries to get the ball to the middle of the field, to allow an opportunity to then attack into either wing. Therefore, good defense keeps the ball away from the middle.

Marking

Another basic of good defense is to "mark" or cover players in one's zone. When the ball is elsewhere, defenders must of course look at the player with the ball and try to anticipate the next move. However, they must also know if there are opposing players in their area and "mark" them. This means that they want to be able to *anticipate a pass* to such a player and *intercept it*, or otherwise be near enough and in position to pressure the player. Sometimes the defender's presence alone will prevent the pass, thus *denying* the ball to their zone. Tell your children to try to think where the pass will go, and get into position to intercept it if in their zone. In front of the goal, unmarked players will often score; they *must* be marked.

Move Out

This is an important concept. We will more formally define the offsides rule in the next chapter, even though we have touched on it previously. It essentially means that forwards can't hang around the goal waiting for a pass. There are only two ways that an offensive player can advance towards the goal: 1) if the ball is closer to the goal than the player is; or 2) if a defensive player other than the goalie is closer to the goal than the offensive player. Therefore, it makes a lot of sense for defensive players not to hang around the goal. If they do, offensive players can do so also. Full-backs on their half of the field want to stay as far upfield as they can, knowing that the forwards on the opposing team can't advance farther than their position without the ball. Of course, the defensive players must fall back as the ball approaches or passes their line, since everybody may always advance at least as far as the ball. Therefore, once the ball is played back upfield, fullbacks will yell, "*Move out,*" heading upfield and forcing forwards to withdraw

Figure 40
OFFSIDES TRAP

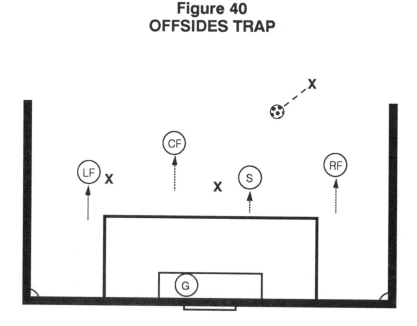

Before (X) plays the ball, all fullbacks and sweeper, on signal, suddenly advance upfield. Then as soon as the ball is passed, the opponent closest to the goal is offsides

with them.

Another defensive strategy then is to use the offsides rule to gain possession of the ball. A fullback downfield of the ball just has to run up past the person he or she is guarding, and as soon as that person affects the play (e.g., a pass is made to them) the referee will blow the whistle, call offsides, and award possession to the defense. The team receiving possession gets a free indirect kick. Make sure another fullback isn't also behind the opposing player, or the trap will not work.

Often teams will call an *offsides trap* wherein a designated player calls the trap and all fullbacks run forward past the offensive players. This is usually done just before an opponent passes the ball forward, resulting in an offside penalty. (See Figure 40.)

Of course, offsides traps can be quite dangerous. If the defensive player does not get past the offensive player before the ball is kicked, then the offensive player may have a free strike on goal. Or, the referee may miss the offsides penalty. In youth soccer,

Figure 41
GET THE BODY BEHIND TRAPS

Often the ball will bounce over or skip under an outstretched toe

Body is balanced and squarely behind approaching ball

Figure 42
MAKE A WALL

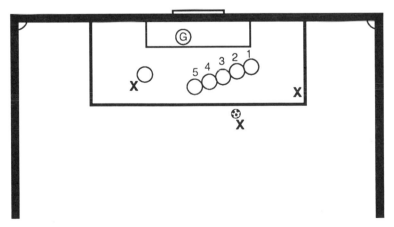

The wall captain (1) lines up between ball and near post. Since the ball is dangerously close he calls for a five man wall, and the players with assigned numbers line up in order

where there is usually only one field referee and no linesmen, this occurs frequently, to a chorus of groans from the parents and fans. Many a game has been decided on a missed offside call. Players should learn to raise their hands upon an offside to get the referee's attention. It's often really hard to see these penalties from a distance. I like to have all fullbacks raise their hands on an offside trap, so the referee is alerted. In any event, they must play the whistle and keep playing if they don't hear it!

Tackle Before the Player has Control

We touched on this in Chapter 4. The best time to attack players with the ball is just as they are trapping it, before they get full control. However, it's even more important to make sure you stay between the ball and the goal.

Don't Kick into an Opposing Player

This will happen and is sometimes hard to avoid. It's deadly when a fullback does it. I've seen goals scored because a fullback kicked a ball into a striking forward, who rebounded it, unintentionally, right into the net. Tell your child to try to pass the ball *around* any opposing player.

Use the Whole Body to Trap

At young ages particularly, the child will stick out a toe or thigh to a bouncing ball and miss it completely. When defending, if there is time, the player should try to get in front of the ball, and trap it fully with the side of the foot, or the body if the ball is in the air. This will minimize missing the ball completely. (See Figure 41.)

Pass to Goalie

A fullback who has no good passing or dribbling option should pass back to the goalie, if he is not too far away. This is a form of safety pass. However, if there is any chance a defender can intercept, it should not be passed. Remember, it's a pass, not a shot! Make it firm and direct but not too hard. I've seen goals scored on this play. I've seen the pass get by the goalie and roll into the net.

It happened to me once! However, it can be a very effective defensive play. The goalie can then punt or pass the ball to an open teammate.

Make a Wall

Upon certain penalties, as discussed further in the next chapter, the referee will award a free direct or indirect kick. If the kick is taken from near the penalty area, there is a good chance to score, so the defense needs to help the goalie by making a human wall. In youth soccer this is often a confused process, and there is no need for it to be.

There are a few simple principles involved: 1) the wall protects the near post goal area, and the goalie covers the far post area; 2) one person is the *captain*, whose responsibility is to organize the wall (working with the goalie and shifting the wall upon the goalie's instructions). The captain lines up on line with the near post, and the other players line up on the captain's inside shoulder; 3) the captain raises a number of fingers to call for the number of players in the wall; 4) shots near the eighteen yard line get five players, and the number drops as distance or angle to the goal increases; 5) players all have assigned numbers, and line up accordingly. If the captain raises four fingers, then the defenders with assigned number two, three, and four join the captain on the line. (See Figure 42.) The wall must be at least ten yards from the ball. It's essential to form walls quickly, and they should be practiced. The offense will try to get the shot off before the wall is formed. Other players who could receive a short pass on the free kick must be marked, and the goalie must ensure that no opponent is unmarked.

9.

RULES OF THE GAME

RULES, FIELD DIMENSIONS, AND TALKING SOCCER

Soccer is a *very* old sport. Stories tell of barbarian soldiers kicking around the skulls of their enemies. It is said to have been played in China and ancient Greece thousands of years ago. It is likely that kids were kicking round things as soon as there were kids and round things. For the last 1000 years in England the game was played, often between two towns, kicking a pig's bladder from a point midway between the towns. Hundreds were involved, and it became quite violent. After a while some rules were formulated although this did not occur until about 1850. One day a player picked up the ball and ran with it, leading to the formation of rugby, and still later, Irish or American style football.

However, to millions of people around the world, what we call soccer is football. Over 130 nations are now members of the world soccer governing body, F.I.F.A. It is clearly the most popular game in the world, and became an Olympic Game in 1908. Now every four years since 1930, as in the Olympics, each nation sends a team of its citizens to vie for the World Cup, the zenith of soccer.

SOCCER: A THUMBNAIL DESCRIPTION

Modern day soccer is a game played upon a flat field up to 130 yards long and 100 yards wide. American soccer fields are usually

Figure 43
SOCCER FIELD DIMENSIONS

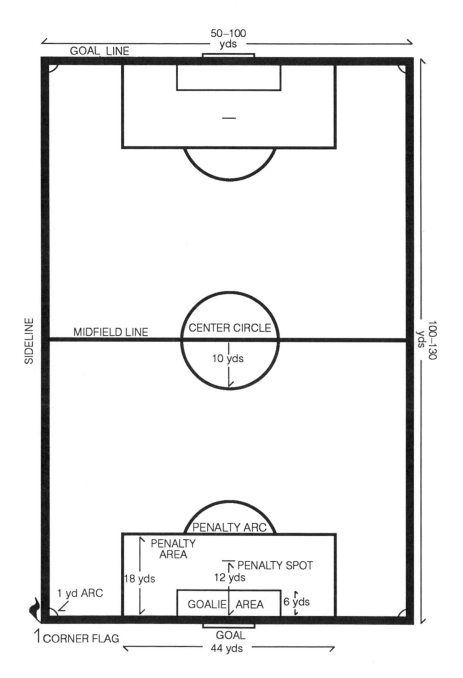

about the size of a football field. Field size is not a critical issue. Smaller kids often play on fields about eighty yards long. "Pick-up" games often occur with only six or seven on a side, so even smaller fields are marked out. A field just needs to be large enough for players to run freely, but not too large or they will tire quickly. At either end of the field is a goal post with sideposts twenty-four feet apart holding up a crossbar eight feet from the ground and backed up by a net. (See Figure 43.)

Two teams of eleven players each, including the goalie, must attempt to score goals by shooting the ball into the opponent's net. Some players try to score, and so they play forward. Some defend and stay back; some play the midfield. A goal is scored when the whole ball is completely past the goal line.

Games last usually for ninety minutes, with teams exchanging sides after forty-five minute halves, with a five minute halftime break. Younger kids play shorter games. Play is continuous and the clock is stopped only for unusual delays such as injuries. The game goes on, rain or shine, unless the field becomes hazardous. Rules on substitutes vary. Usually subs come in at the half or midway through the half. Sometimes they are allowed upon any referee's whistle stopping action, or on any out of bounds.

Players may receive and advance the ball with any part of their bodies except the arms; upper shoulders are okay.

When a player kicks the ball out of bounds on the side of the field, the opposing team may throw it back into play at the point it left the field.

Upon any *intentional* penalty, such as striking the opponent, touching the ball with the hand or arm (a *handball*), offsides, or kicking the ball past the end line, the opposing team is awarded a free kick. Intentional fouls or hand balls may be directly kicked towards goal. Offsides or minor fouls, such as obstruction or dangerous play, are awarded indirect kicks which must be touched by two players before a score can be allowed. A serious foul in the penalty area results in a penalty shot on goal. Limited physical contact with the shoulder or hip (no arms!) is allowed so long as the player is playing the ball.

The goalie may use hands in the penalty area, and may not be interfered with in the goal area. Upon catching the ball up to four steps may be taken before the ball must then be punted or thrown outside of the penalty area. Once the goalie possesses the ball, it may not be kicked from his hands.

That's soccer! It's a very uncomplicated game. There are not as many rules as most American sports. Its beauty is in its simplicity. Kids get to kick a ball around, and try to score, and that's about it. There are a few complications, such as the offside rule and when free kicks are given. There is a rule that allows a referee to ignore a foul if the fouled team has an *advantage*, e.g. the fouled player is advancing towards goal and keeps possession notwithstanding the foul. *Throw-ins* have a funny sort of rule on how they are to be handled. But that's about it.

Figure 44
SOCCER BALLS

Pictured next to a basketball, for comparison, are a size 5, a size 4, a size 1½, and a hackey-sack sits atop the basketball

GLOSSARY: TALKING SOCCER

The following glossary, "talking soccer," covers the main rules in detail and much of the language of soccer. I've already covered much of the game in preceding chapters so I will not duplicate everything here.

BALL—Soccer balls come in three basic sizes. Size 5 is the primary official regulation, and is twenty-seven to twenty-eight inches in circumference, about an inch in diameter smaller than a basketball, and fourteen to sixteen ounces in weight. Size 4 is smaller by a few inches and a few ounces, and is used for kids below about twelve years of age. Size 3 is for tiny tots! The ball should always be properly inflated, otherwise it could lead to injury. It is *essential* for your child to own a ball. Any old ball will do, there is no need to spend a lot of money. Practice is critical and can't be done without a ball. Your local soccer club may buy them in bulk and give you a good deal on one. Owning a few balls is useful, if you can pick them up, even if they are used (try a garage sale). It saves a lot of time to have extra balls when practicing. I use a *volleyball* for heading practice for younger kids. The little *hackey sacks* are fun too. (See Figure 44.)

BICYCLE—A fancy play where a player falls backward kicking the ball when upside down to a point behind him. I've never taught it, as it is dangerous.

BREAK AWAY—When a striker or wing breaks away from a defender and charges the goalie one-on-one. An excellent chance to score.

CENTER PASS—To pass the ball towards the center of the field in front of the goal. It's the bread-and-butter play of soccer offense.

CENTER CIRCLE—A ten yard radius circle in the middle of the field where play starts at the beginning of each half and after each goal. Defenders may not enter the circle until the ball rolls one full turn.

CENTER LINE—The line which divides the field in half, parallel to the goal lines.

CLEAR—A hard defensive kick, *clearing* the ball from the area in front of the goal. This is usually a desperation kick to no one in particular, when under pressure. At young ages you often hear the coach shrieking this word when the ball is in front of the goal!

CORNER KICK—Whenever the ball goes out of bounds past the goal line and was last touched by a defensive player, the opponent is awarded a free direct kick. The ball is placed within a small pie-shaped area with a one yard radius, at the corner of the field nearest to where the ball went out of bounds. The player kicks the ball hard, just below the center, and tries to place it near the goal. Sometimes a player can curve the ball right into the goal. The other teammates usually bunch up and charge the goal to the area where the ball will be kicked. Usually a tall player tries to head it in. The defense positions players at each goal post and other defenders mark forwards as they charge. The goalie's decision is whether or not to leap to the ball and grab it from the air.

COIN TOSS—The winner chooses to kick off or defend the goal of choice. In a strong wind it is often advantageous to choose the upwind goal instead of the ball, particularly since the wind may later die down. A strong wind seems to add a few players to the team which has it at its back.

CHARGE—The shoulder charge is a legal play, jarring the player with the ball, so long as the arm does not touch the player, and so long as one is playing the ball upon contact. If too hard or dangerous, the referee will award a free kick.

DIRECT KICK—See PENALTIES.

DINK—Actually a volleyball term, it's a soft chip shot over a charging goalie's head.

DROP BALL—This does not occur often, but when the referee does not know who last touched the ball out of bounds, or after an injury during play, play begins again with a drop ball, similar to the face-off in hockey. The ball is dropped between two players and all others must stay ten yards away.

FAR POST—If your child is a shooter, then these two words should be emblazoned upon his or her mind. Usually, try to shoot between the far post, the goal post farthest from the shooter, and the goalie. If the shot misses, it allows for a second chance by teammates, and it also allows more time for the ball to curve into the goal.

FINISH—How often do we hear a coach lament that a kid can attack but can't finish, that is, execute a shot or a center pass while in a dead run?

FLAGS—At the four corners of the field there are flags which are at least five feet high, marking the corners.

FORWARDS—Offensive players. Shooters. Fast, good dribblers, can shoot or pass on the run. There are wing forwards, center forwards, inside forwards, and strikers.

FREE KICKS—Goal kicks, penalty kicks, corner kicks, and direct and indirect kicks. The main strategy for all free kicks, awarded upon various violations, is to move quickly, catching the defense off guard. Similarly, the defense, which naturally tends to relax upon stoppage of play, must hustle to defend the free kick, forming a wall if near goal.

FULLBACKS—Defensive players. Big, strong, aggressive. There are wing fullbacks, center fullbacks, sweepers, and stoppers.

GIVE AND GO—An essential offensive maneuver involving a short pass to a teammate and a quick pass back as the first player sprints past the defender; also called a *wall pass*.

GOAL KICK—A free kick awarded to the defense when an offensive player kicks the ball out of bounds beyond the goal line. It must be taken from within the goal area on the side from which the ball went out of bounds. It must exit the penalty area before any player can play the ball. At young ages the kick should be to the corner of the penalty area since kicks to the middle carry a high risk of interception at a very dangerous spot. Often a goalie kicks it to an unmarked player close to the penalty area perimeter who then shovels it back to the goalie. The goalie may then punt or throw the ball upfield.

HALFBACKS—Play the middle of the field. Good skills, endurance runners. There are wing or side halfbacks, center halfbacks, midfielders, and linkmen.

INJURY—A player injured, unable to play, and sitting on the ground. Referee may, after allowing the opponent full advantage of a possession stop play, allow the injury to be examined, and allow substitution.

KICKOFF—The opening movement of each soccer half and after each score. The opposing players must remain outside the

Figure 45
KICKOFF

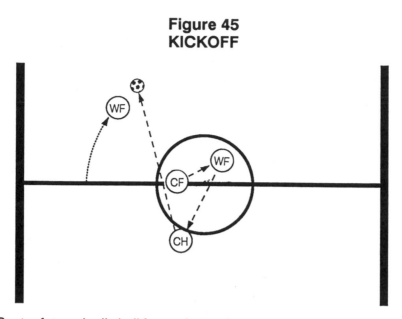

Center forward rolls ball forward to a winger who in turn shovels it back to the center half. She then passes it up strongly to the other wing forward.

center circle until the ball has advanced forward a distance equal to the ball's circumference. A typical kickoff has two forwards in the circle, one rolls it to the other who then kicks the ball back to the center halfback who then kicks up to a wing for a possible wing attack. Defensive players, especially halfbacks, should pick up any wings who penetrate their area during a kickoff, and anticipate the pass. (See Figure 45.)

LINESMAN—Usually you will not see these officials until high school or championship play. They roam the sidelines with a small flag in hand to signal the referee when the ball goes out of bounds, or when they see an offside or other infraction. The final call is the referee's.

MARK—To defend against a particular person, to stay close by him. This *must* be done to any offensive player in the penalty area. Also called man-to-man defense.

MATCH—A soccer game.

MIDFIELD—The middle third of a soccer field.

OFFSIDE—The rule books say that a player is offside if

nearer the opponent's goal line than the ball is at the moment the ball is played toward the player by a teammate, unless a) the player is on one's own half of the field; or b) two defenders (including the goalie) are nearer the goal line than the attacker; or c) the offensive player receives the ball on a goal kick, corner kick, throw-in, or drop ball. This all means that offensive players cannot just hang around the opposing goalie, waiting for a pass. They have to have the ball; or a defender plus the goalie has to be inside them. You basically have to *earn* forward progress with the ball. Defenders can use this rule effectively to stop forwards from penetrating. It must be taught and repeated constantly! This rule is the source of many a groan at soccer games. It is often missed if there are no linesmen, and some referees ignore or misunderstand the part about not being offside *at the time the ball is kicked.* Often a player will move past his defender as soon as the ball is in flight, and will erroneously be called offside.

OVERLAP—Movement of players past other teammates to receive a pass, to advance the ball.

PENALTIES—Soccer today is a game associated with much fan violence, demonstrating the passion with which it is regarded around the world. However, at one time the violence was very much on the field. Games were often a rumble between villages, with hundreds of players on a side, and with no rules. It got so bad that King Edward banned games in 1314. However, in the late 1800's a number of rules emerged to remove violence from the field of play.

Upon a violation, the referee may stop play. However, if the team violated has possession of the ball, the referee may allow them the *advantage.* This means the referee thinks it's better for them to *play on* than to receive a free kick.

When play is blown dead, the referee signals whether the award is a *direct kick,* by pointing his hand towards goal, or an *indirect kick,* by pointing his hand straight up. The referee's other hand usually points to the spot where the kick must be taken.

A direct kick means that the kicker may score by shooting directly at goal. In an indirect kick, another player must touch the ball before a goal can be scored. Defensive players must stand ten yards away from the kicker on all free kicks. If close to the goal the defense often forms a human wall to protect the goal.

A *penalty kick* is awarded for a violation which would result in a direct kick from within the penalty area. The shot is taken from a point twelve yards from the center of the goal. All other players must remain outside the penalty area. The goalie must have both feet on the goal line until the ball is kicked. The kicker or a teammate may take additional shots upon a rebound touched by the goalie (a rebound off the goal post not touched by the goalie is a dead ball).

Direct kicks are awarded upon intentional fouls such as kicking, jumping, striking, tripping, holding, pushing another player, or intentionally touching the ball with the hand or arm.

Indirect kicks are awarded for unintentional fouls, or for obstruction, dangerous play such as raising the foot high, dangerously lowering one's head, ungentlemanly behavior, abusive language, kicking the ball when on the ground, or kicking a ball held by the goalkeeper.

The referee may additionally *warn* a player or coach by holding a *yellow card* in the air, or expel a player or coach from the game by holding a *red card* into the air. Two warnings equal a red card. Red cards often carry a suspension for additional games.

PENETRATION—Getting deep into the defense in preparation for an attack on goal. Wings and strikers must always endeavor to penetrate as far as the offside rule allows. How often do we see a nice pass to open space, into the wing, but no forward up far enough to get to it. Forwards must stay forward. Tell them to let the halfbacks get the ball up to them.

PITCH—An English term for a soccer field.

PRESSURE—The heart of good defense is to pressure the ball carrier in any and every way allowable. Often just running toward a player will cause that player to pass errantly.

RUN OFF THE BALL—Getting into position to help the team when one does not have possession of the ball. To try to run to or create open space.

SERVE—To pass the ball, just another term.

SHOES—The most important piece of equipment is good soccer shoes. Get a cheap ball if you must, but don't get cheap shoes. The ball control surfaces should be smooth. Cleats are absolutely necessary for balance and changing direction quickly. Cleats cannot be pointy, and must be at least 1/2 inch wide and no more than 3/4 inch deep. I recommend high-top shoes, since sprained ankles are so common in soccer.

SHIN GUARDS—For some reason these are not required equipment, and they should be at all youth levels. When bones are broken, it's usually from getting kicked in the shin area. They are inexpensive, and are a must as far as I'm concerned.

SMALL-SIDED GAME—A practice game of between three to six players on a side, usually played sideways on the field, using cones, four to six feet apart, as goals. A good rule, since there is no goalie, is that the ball must travel below knee height when scoring. I believe that small children should never play more than seven on a side, because the larger numbers overwhelm them. We throw them into eleven player teams much too soon!

SQUARE—A lateral pass.

TACKLE—To steal the ball from a dribbler.

THROUGH—A pass past the defense for a teammate to run to, usually a wing.

TIE-BREAKER—A relatively recent innovation employed to break ties. Five players on the field at game's end from each team are selected to take penalty shots. The team that scores most wins. If, after all ten shots, the score is still tied, sudden death commences with the sixth player. Even more recent is the *shootout*, where the player starts from well outside the penalty area and is given five seconds to score. The goalie can move at will.

TOUCH—Contact with the ball. One-touch means you receive and pass in the same single contact. Two-touch means to trap it and immediately pass it with the next touch.

TRAP—To receive a pass or otherwise collect a moving ball.

VOLLEY—Kicking a ball in flight in midair.

WALL—Line of defenders, shoulder to shoulder, who deflect free kicks.

10.
ODDS AND ENDS

BOYS AND GIRLS TOGETHER

Soccer is a universal game. That's why it's the most popular game in the world. I think, based on all of my years as a coach and a player of various sports, that soccer is the overall best game there is for kids. Everyone can play, tall, short, boy, girl, fast, slow. It conditions the body very well and is a very even and fluid game.

Girls' soccer has grown tremendously. The traditional women's spring sport, field hockey, is being slowly replaced by soccer. Why it is that women in many countries outside America do not usually play soccer is beyond me. There is no good reason why girls shouldn't play. My first experience as a soccer coach was with my daughter's team, and it was the greatest coaching experience of my life.

Some parents worry about letting their daughters play. One father asked me how to handle the "menstrual situation." I don't need to handle it, in fact in five years of coaching girls I never had an incident. Of course, occasionally a girl would indicate to me she "didn't feel good" and wanted to sit down. I tried to stay alert to that. I had my daughter tell them to tell her whenever cramps or weakness came on too strong. Some studies on women in sports indicate that most women function just as well during their menstrual cycle as otherwise. Modern day pads are excellent in controlling blood flow, so there is usually little problem. Parents shouldn't worry about it. You can intercede, mention a particular problem time to the coach, if your daughter feels uneasy doing it herself.

Figure 46
FEMALE CHEST TRAP

At young ages, some officials will allow girls to protect themselves by trapping with the forearms. Not enough allow it, unfortunately

The chest trap is of some concern, for obvious reasons. Some leagues, however, in order to protect the breast, allow girls to cover themselves by crossing their arms, palms placed downward near their shoulders, elbows and forearms against the abdomen. Check to see if your local club allows this and, if so, you can tell your daughter to practice it. (See Figure 46.)

It doesn't hurt to urge your daughter to engage in some extra conditioning—neck bridges, sit-ups, squats. Little girls often are encouraged to play house while little boys play king of the hill. I know this is changing, but some additional conditioning may be needed in your daughter's case; consider it. Girls' soccer tends to be less physical than boys', but not that much less. Also, I see less heading among girls. This relates I believe to conditioning needs of the neck area.

WARMUPS AND CONDITIONING

For a non-contact sport, soccer has a lot of injuries. This is due to the sudden jerking movements, from getting kicked, or from collisions. Many injuries can be avoided by warmups and proper conditioning.

Muscles are like bubble-gum. If you stretch them slowly, they expand; stretch too quickly and they tear. So warm up. Even if you and your child just go out to kick the ball around, do some warmups.

I recommend starting with a slow jog of several hundred yards. Then do some toe-touches, roll the head around to loosen the neck, do some trunk twists, and jumping jacks. Do a few sit-ups and push-ups if the ground is dry. Stretch the upper leg as much as possible. (See Figure 47.)

I would suggest avoiding weight training at young ages, at least until high school age. Jogging, wind sprints, calisthenics (push-ups, partial knee bends, chin-ups, sit-ups, neck bridges) are quite sufficient. There is one weight exercise I like which is called the extension lift. It's usually a mechanism attached to a bench press machine which allows one, in a seated position, to extend the bent leg straightaway with weight. Use only enough weight so that three repetitions of fifteen each can be done. This exercise increases kicking strength.

INJURIES

No matter how well conditioned a team, injuries can occur anytime. A common injury is a hamstring pull, but these usually don't occur until high school or later ages. Upper leg (groin) strains, sprained ankles, bloody noses, and bruises are common to youth soccer. Thankfully, broken bones are rare, but not rare enough.

Abrasions usually occur when a child falls and scrapes the side of the leg. These are the most likely cuts to get infected. Wash the wound as soon as possible, with soap if handy. Apply a sterile

Figure 47
WARMUPS

Jumping Jacks

Cross legged toe touch

Lower thigh stretch

In this position, lean forward for hamstring and lean back for upper leg

dressing when you are able to, the sooner the better! Just put some antiseptic ointment on it. If it gets red, pussy, or red tracks appear, see a physician immediately.

Lacerations are deeper wounds. Unless bleeding is severe, wash the wound, and apply slight pressure with a bandage to stop the bleeding. If severe, seek first aid. Apply pressure and a large bandage. Immediately elevate the wound higher than the heart to slow bleeding. If the bandage gets blood-soaked apply another on top of it. Don't remove the first one. Care for shock by elevating legs unless you suspect a head or neck injury. In this case don't move the child. If the laceration is minor, a butterfly bandage will hold the skin together. Consult a physician immediately if you suspect stitches are needed.

Contusions and bruises occur frequently. Apply ice quickly, after handling any abrasion or lacerations. Ice will arrest internal bleeding and prevent or lessen swelling. Ice is the best first-aid to have available for nearly any swelling from bruises or sprains. Apply it very quickly, within minutes, and much internal damage will be spared.

Sprained ankles or wrists should be immobilized. An ice pack should be applied immediately. Act as if there is a fracture until you're sure there is no fracture. Call the ambulance if there is any question in your mind. Get an X-ray to see if there is a break or other damage.

If there is a fracture, immobilize the child completely as soon as possible. No movement at all. Be comforting, keep the player warm with coats or blankets, and get medical help. *Do not allow your child to be moved or cared for by anyone who is not medically trained.* If in the middle of the field during a championship game, the game can wait! Insist on this. Permanent damage can result from aggravating a break.

If your child ever falls to the ground *unconscious*, see if anyone has been trained in first aid. The first move, once it is clear that the child will not respond, is to check for vital signs—breathing and pulse. If either are missing, send for an ambulance and have someone trained administer rescue breathing or cardio-pulmonary resuscitation (CPR). Try to stay calm and let the first-aid workers do their job. In all my years of coaching four sports, and playing even more, I've never seen it needed. I hope you won't either.

Finally, *heat exhaustion* can occur easily during a soccer match. The body gets clammy and pale. Remove the child from the game, into shade or a cool spot. Apply cool towels, elevate the feet. If the body temperature is very high and pupils are constricted, you should suspect heat stroke. Call an ambulance and cool the child down fast. Care for shock.

Knees are tough injuries. Often the injury will require some sort of arthroscopic surgery to mend cartilage. Modern procedures are quite advanced, and simple. Have your child see a knowledgeable sports doctor. Your team's coach or high school athletic director will know one.

Tell your child to play the game safely. Aggressiveness is okay, but be careful not to hurt someone. Your hope is that other parents do the same. I play every weekend and there are often one or two guys who take chances with another's health. Don't encourage your child to grow up to be one of them.

When injury occurs, insist on rest. I've seen many kids rush back from a sprained ankle, only to have the injury plague them through the years. Don't let it happen! Make sure your child wears an ankle brace from then on. There are excellent ankle braces on the market today. Get one.

The point is that injuries need time to heal properly. If you give the time, the future can have many years of sport for your child. If you don't, it could be over already.

HOW TO ACT AT GAMES

The worst thing you can do is go to a soccer game and scream your head off. How often I have seen groups of parents by the sidelines screaming at the players, giving directions, and generally raising a ruckus. The scene is a clear one: some poor kid is running up to a loose ball, and parents are screaming, "Get the ball! Get the ball!" Believe me, the kid already knows that! Unfortunately, the screaming focuses his mind more on the ball, when he or she really needs to be looking around at who to pass to. Actually, it's best just to congratulate nice play, and be quiet. The kids on the field or the coach should be communicating to the player about the options. A lot of screaming parents telling players what to do is just confusing. Sometimes the referee will caution against sideline coaching.

If you can't contain yourself, then try to say things that will be helpful. Messages must be clear and concise. For instance, if your child is dribbling and a defender approaches from the rear, yell "man on." If a teammate is free laterally, yell "square." If the wing is breaking forward towards open space, yell "wing" or "through." If no one is near the player, yell "settle" if the child is trapping the ball. Suggest there is time to get control. "Run with it," "walk the dog," "dribble," "penetrate," or "carry it," suggest there is time to advance by dribbling the ball.

If there is great pressure and no obvious passing opportunity, then yell "back," or "drop it" to suggest a pass back to an open player.

If a wing is advancing the ball into the wing corner, then remind that player to "center" the ball if the striker is approaching the goal area.

If it's windy and the wind is against your team, remind them to keep passes low, on the ground. If it's a cross wind, then remind them to avoid kicking out of bounds.

Remind your defenders to slow down the opposing strikers, and to try to trap offside or move out. If there are undefended offensive players in the goal area, yell for someone to "mark the middle." If the ball is in front of the goal yell for fullbacks to "clear" it away.

If your team has the ball in the other team's goal area, remind your forwards to "think net," and shoot at the "far post."

Yell helpful things like "give and go" or "run off the ball" or "make open space."

Always be reasonable. Don't confuse the kids. If things are getting loud and hectic, then say nothing. Follow the coach's lead, don't give confusing messages. At young ages, the kids need the help, but not confusion. They tend to bunch up, "swarm soccer" I call it. Remind them to spread out.

Most important, be positive. Don't criticize anyone, especially your child. Don't take out your frustrations on the kid who makes a mistake. It embarrasses both of you, and it only teaches the child to play less confidently. I guarantee they will all make mistakes, for years, and they will not improve if you punctuate mistakes with things like, "What's the matter with you?", or "That was stupid!" If you cannot control yourself then stay home. This may sound tough, but you will do a lot of damage to your child, and to your relationship with your child if you don't control anger. I've seen this problem often, and it really can screw a kid up.

HOW TO TREAT THE COACH

First of all, the coach is giving up a lot of time, and deserves a lot of room. If you want to coach, sign up to do so or to help. Show up at practices, and offer to help. That earns you the right to have an opinion. Otherwise, be very conservative about offering it.

Second, realize your bias. You are a parent, and love your child. You may think he deserves to play more or to play another position. But the coach knows a lot more about what kids can do, and who has earned playing time. It's unfair for you to ask for more, and unfair to the other kids to, in effect, suggest that one of them should play less. Work more with your child, foster improvement, and more playing time will follow. Coaches want to win, and they usually will give the better players more playing time.

However, coaches need to learn too. And sometimes they go about things quite wrong. If this is the case, then gently indicate how you feel. It's important that you think about it a lot, and make sure you know what you are talking about. Question your own biases. If you feel you can help, offer your opinion about it. Avoid an argument, even a long debate. Make your point, ask the coach to think about it. Indicate you are only trying to help. I would strongly suggest not being argumentative. Say your piece, listen to the coach, then thank him for his time and end it. If you're lucky, the coach will be thankful, but he may resent your interference and possibly even take it out on your child. If the situation becomes very bad, let your club president or coordinator know how you feel. Keep in mind that your child may suffer if caught in the middle of it. If the experience is more damaging than good, then remove your child from the team. But remember to think about it, get advice, talk to other parents, avoid being unduly disruptive.

11.

PARENT'S CHECKLIST

Now that you have read the book, it's time to get outside and have some fun with your child. I find it useful when I coach to have a checklist of things I want to remember during practice. So here is a checklist for you to use. Keep saying these things over and over.

KNOWING THE BALL

Know the ball. Fool around with it. Know how it reacts to different contacts. Keep it nearby.

DRIBBLING

- ✓ Use both feet.
- ✓ Keep the eyes up.
- ✓ Sweep the ball, do not strike it.
- ✓ Keep it close for control.
- ✓ Maintain body balance.
- ✓ Use head and body fakes.
- ✓ Explode to open space.
- ✓ Drills: Slalom with cones, speed dribble, one-on-one in a box.

JUGGLING

- ✓ Use feet, thigh, head, and chest.
- ✓ Concentrate on the bottom of the ball.
- ✓ Don't juggle too high at first.
- ✓ Do one better each time.

PASSING

✓ Know where your nearest teammates are.
✓ Pass in front of the receiver with appropriate ball speed.
✓ Settle the ball down before passing.
✓ Hop and plant the non-kicking foot at the side of the ball.
✓ Kicking the knee over the ball, point toe down, lock the ankle.
✓ Use inside, outside, or instep depending on direction and distance from the target.
✓ Kick with leg speed.
✓ Follow through.
✓ Move on contact.
✓ Drills: Have a catch, wall kicking.

RECEIVING THE PASS

✓ Practice juggling.
✓ Get to the ball. It's a foot race.
✓ Meet the ball. Don't wait for it.
✓ Take command of the ball. Don't let it play you.
✓ Face the ball and present a body surface.
✓ Relax upon contact. Don't get excited.
✓ Deaden surface and withdraw. Go limp.
✓ Decide where to drop the ball. Where is the defender?
✓ Volley if need be.
✓ Move on contact.
✓ Drills: Wall kicking, two person drill, keep away, showdown.

THROW-INS

✓ Try to throw it up along the sideline.
✓ Be ready for a pass back.
✓ Throw forward, from over the head, with both hands evenly in one motion, with both feet on the ground.

HEADING

✓ Concentrate, keep the eyes open.
✓ Make contact with the forehead.
✓ Neck rigid, body balanced.
✓ Arch back and thrust head to pass.
✓ Jump for high balls, hinge waist, swing legs forward.

FIELD POSITIONS

- ✓ **Forwards:** Speed, good dribbler, desire to score, need to execute center pass on a dead run.
- ✓ **Fullbacks:** Big, strong, aggressive, fearless. Need to delay penetration, don't overcommit, hold ground.
- ✓ **Halfbacks:** Best skills, distance runners, need to do throw-ins and be able to turn with the ball.
- ✓ **Goalie:** Top athlete. Good hands. Leader.

OFFENSE

- ✓ Overlap. Play total soccer.
- ✓ Attack from the wings.
- ✓ Give and go.
- ✓ Safety pass back.
- ✓ Flow with the ball.
- ✓ Create or move to open space.
- ✓ Wings stay wide.
- ✓ Square. Pass to center.
- ✓ Switch positions.
- ✓ Encourage shots.
- ✓ Run with the ball when you can.

DEFENSE

- ✓ Pursuit.
- ✓ Contain, apply pressure, but don't overcommit.
- ✓ Keep the ball wide.
- ✓ Mark free players.
- ✓ Don't hang around goal.
- ✓ Offsides rule. Offsides trap.
- ✓ Don't kick into opposing player.
- ✓ Tackle before player has control.
- ✓ Use whole body to trap.
- ✓ Pass to goalie if needed.
- ✓ Make a wall on free kicks.

A TYPICAL PRACTICE SESSION

The practice session will depend on the age of the players.

The main variable is how much to focus on skills as opposed to dynamics and field play. At young ages more basics are needed. There is no sense in teaching play patterns if they can't pass or trap.

I used to start my teams with warmups, as detailed earlier in this chapter. Then, while they were catching their breath, I'd talk about something—the last game, the next game, a concept such as *the wing attack*.

Then we would do *stations*. The fifteen players would be divided into five groups of three each. I'd divide the field into five areas or stations, each involving a skill drill such as:

Station 1: Slalom Dribbling—using cones.

Station 2: Trapping. Players would throw the ball to each other, at varying heights, forcing use of different body surfaces.

Station 3: Speed Dribbling—about thirty yards, finishing up with a pass on the run.

Station 4: Monkey in the Middle. Three players in a 20-foot square marked off by cones.

Station 5: Heading Practice.

I'd place a parent to supervise each station. I'd include other drills on other days such as: one on one, two players fighting for a loose ball, juggling, king of the hill, throw-ins, half-turns.

Each group would stay at the station for five minutes, and then I would rotate all groups among the stations. In twenty-five minutes each group would have participated in all stations.

During the second half hour we would work on dynamics. The forwards and center halfback would repeatedly attack a goal defended by two players, working out the patterns of a wing attack, center pass, give and go. We would work on corner kicks, making a wall to defend direct kicks, kickoffs, throw-ins.

Then we would finish up with soccer. They would divide up for a small-sided game. I would play too! Parents would play! Other times we played a variation of baseball/kickball, where players must kick the rolled pitch as hard as they could and circle bases. The defending team would need to score a goal before the runner got "home." The runner could leave the basepath, retrieve the ball, and put it away again, then return to circling the bases. It was hilarious! Always end practice with something fun!

That's it. That's all I know. Good luck!

INDEX

More Great Books in the *Parent's Guide* series!

Your influence as a coach or teacher can give children (both yours and others) the greatest gifts of all: strong self-confidence and high self-esteem. The *Parent's Guide* series has nearly a dozen books full of helpful illustrations and step-by-step guides on how to nurture and encourage children as they strive for success in sports and the arts. Plus, the friendly, familiar tone of each book will help both you and the child have fun as you learn.

The Parent's Guide to Coaching Baseball — #70076/$7.95/128 pages/paperback

The Parent's Guide to Coaching Basketball — #70077/$7.95/136 pages/paperback

The Parent's Guide to Coaching Football — #70078/$7.95/144 pages/paperback

The Parent's Guide to Coaching Hockey — #70216/$8.95/176 pages/paperback

The Parent's Guide to Coaching Physically Challenged Children — #70255/$12.95/ 144 pages/paperback

The Parent's Guide to Coaching Soccer — #70079/$8.95/136 pages/paperback

The Parent's Guide to Coaching Tennis — #70080/$7.95/144 pages/paperback

The Parent's Guide to Coaching Skiing — #70217/$8.95/144 pages/paperback

The Parent's Guide to Teaching Music — #70082/$7.95/136 pages/paperback

The Parent's Guide to Band and Orchestra — #70075/$7.95/136 pages/paperback

The Parent's Guide to Teaching Art: How to Encourage Your Child's Artistic Talent and Ability — #70081/$11.95/184 pages/paperback

The Parent's Guide to Teaching Self-Defense — #70254/$12.95/144 pages/paperback